CHILDREN'S art & crafts

The Australian Women's Weekly Home Library

Author:
NANCY LEWIS BARTLETT

Editor:
SUE WENDT

Production editor:
MARYANNE BLACKER

Art director:
ROBBYLEE PHELAN

ACP Editor in chief:
TREVOR KENNEDY

ACP Deputy Editor in chief:
DAWN SWAIN

Produced by the Australian Women's Weekly Home Library Division
Typeset by Photoset Computer Service Pty Ltd, Sydney, Australia
Printed by Dai Nippon Co Ltd, Tokyo, Japan
Published by Australian Consolidated Press, 54 Park Street, Sydney
Distributed by Network Distribution Company, 54 Park Street, Sydney
Distributed in UK by T.B. Clarke (UK) Ltd (0604) 23 0941

Contents

The importance of creative play for children is easily underestimated. Art and craft projects can excite even the youngest child's imagination and promote a sense of great achievement.

This book presents step-by-step projects that simplify preparation and clean-up and encourage creativity. Emphasis is given to projects for younger children, aged from two to eight. Older children may take simple projects further, without being continually supervised.

The book will help parents and grandparents, teachers of young children, play group supervisors and those who train teachers. In short, anyone who spends time with children.

The projects have been chosen carefully to assist children in the growth of many skills, including small muscle development, hand-eye co-ordination, sensory discrimination, concentration, how to solve problems and make decisions.

Use this book as a guide to develop your child's confidence and pride in his or her own ideas. If a child tends to copy exactly the illustrations, put the book away. Encourage children to experiment — they need to know there is no one right way for their art work to look when finished. Self-expression should be fun!

Nancy Lewis Bartlett

NANCY LEWIS BARTLETT has received numerous art scholarships and holds a Master's Degree in Child Development. For a number of years she taught early childhood education courses at several American universities, including the University of California, where she was director of the child care centre. She lives now with her husband Richard in Canberra, A.C.T., where their seven children were born.

Guidelines
What you'll need (and need to know)

Every preschool, kindergarten, community group or family where young children are involved in art and crafts will need certain basic items, although adults can use great ingenuity when providing the tools for creativity. Always look for supplies at variety and discount shops. However, when quality and safety are important, as with scissors, items should be sought in shops specialising in these requirements. Don't overlook though the endless variety of environmental nature materials that can be used for art and craft projects.

Age: we have suggested a minimum age for most projects as a guide to those that may prove too difficult for younger children. ALL AGES means from two years upwards but obviously requires supervision. The ages given are a guide only as children differ in their ability to master certain steps. With close supervision, younger children may be able to manage, although their attention span may not last until the project is finished. We have used the word (adult) to show where help is needed for very young children, or where toxic products are to be used, or cooking or heating is required.

Coloured chalk: avoid hard, scratchy chalk. Soft, brightly coloured chalk is relatively inexpensive and available from children's supplies stores.

Crayons should be at least 13mm in diameter for children under 5 to use. Small thin crayons break easily and are difficult for little fingers to grip.

Glitter is easiest to use in a coarse salt shaker. Put a sheet of newspaper under the shaker. Shake the excess glitter onto the newspaper. Lift each side so that the glitter falls to the fold in the newspaper. Put one end of the fold onto the edge of the open salt shaker and lift paper to allow glitter to fall into shaker.

Newsprint Paper: this is cheap and comes in colours. Try to find at least the 40cm × 60cm size. It absorbs liquid more than other paper and tears more easily. Ideal for easel painting. Available from local printers' supply shop.

Oil pastels are smooth and vividly coloured and give the effect of oily chalk.

Papier mâché is a technique where pulped paper soaked in wallpaper paste is moulded into shapes, or where objects are covered with strips of paper dipped into wallpaper paste and left to dry.

Scissors: cheap scissors are a waste of money because soon they will not cut without tearing. Spend a little more money on small scissors with a blunt end. Left-handed scissors are available at school supply shops.

Staplers: use medium size staplers, about 10cm to 15cm, because purse size staplers break easily and large staplers are too hard for children to press down.

PASTE AND GLUE

Clear craft glue is more expensive than P.V.A. glue and not as strong, although it's faster drying. It is particularly helpful in holding fabrics and laces in place, but will seep through fabrics if applied too liberally. It is harmful if eaten or inhaled.

Commercial liquid starch can be purchased already made up in many stores. It has an indefinite storage life.

Commercial paper paste: any sort will do but the most vivid colours are achieved from paper paste made for lightweight wallpapers, hobbies and crafts. Follow the directions using cold water and stirring briskly while adding the powder and for a minute afterwards. It often has lumps at first, but these usually disappear in a few hours. This is made up quickly, has no fungicide, is non-toxic and lasts for several days when kept in an airtight container. A 50 gram bag will make 4 litres.

Cornflour mixture is used as an alternative to paper paste as it is usually in the pantry. In a saucepan add 2 tablespoons of cornflour to enough cold water to form a paste. Add about 1 cup of cold water and cook on stove until it reaches a custard consistency. Add more warm water if a thinner consistency is desired. Store in refrigerator as it spoils in hot weather.

Extra strong homemade liquid starch: dissolve 1 tablespoon of granulated starch and follow instructions for Homemade commercial strength liquid starch.

Flour paste: add ½ cup flour to ¾ cup cold water to make a thin paste. Boil several minutes over slow heat until thick, stirring constantly. Add a few drops of oil of cloves, wintergreen or peppermint as preservatives. Thin with cold water. Store in airtight container in refrigerator.

Homemade commercial strength liquid starch: dissolve 1 teaspoon of granulated starch in a small amount of water. While stirring, add 1 cup of hot water. Bring to the boil for 1 minute, stirring constantly. Cool. Store in airtight container in refrigerator. Longlasting.

Liquid starch is very useful for gluing paper. It dries clear and sticks to glass, metal, waxed paper, plastics. Occasionally commercial mixed liquid strength is not thick enough.

P.V.A. glue is mentioned extensively in this book; it stands for poly vinyl adhesive and is widely available. If using P.V.A. glue a lot, put an old lino square underneath project for easier clean up.

PAINT

When the type of paint is not specified but listed as "paint", any sort of non-toxic paint will do. Always store it in an airtight container. Have children wear aprons while painting and keep a bucket of soapy water and sponges on hand.

Brushes should be from 1½cm to 10cm wide and have long handles (over 15cm). Occasionally fine pointed brushes are needed for a particular project. They should be cleaned in cold water and soap after use and stored in a can with their bristles up, or wrapped in newspaper. If possible, use a separate brush for each different colour.

Edicol is a harmless vegetable food dye in powder form. It is expensive and generally bought in bulk by preschools — one standard kilogram tin of colour is enough to last a school for several years and a family for generations. It comes in brilliant blue (aqua), carmine blue (dull), red, yellow, and green. The colours can be mixed to make new colours. The dye is made by placing about 1 tablespoon of water in a container and adding ⅛ of a teaspoon of dye powder and stirring. Add more dye for a more intense colour. Edicol can be purchased at children's educational toy shops. Food colouring can be used as a substitute.

Edicol paint is made by dissolving about ⅛ of a teaspoon of dye powder in a tablespoon of water and adding it to wallpaper paste, a cornflour mixture or liquid starch. The colours are most brilliant and translucent when mixed with paper paste designed for hobbies and crafts. It does not cover lettering on boxes or newsprint as well as powder tempera paint does.

Food colouring is widely available in liquid form from supermarkets and health food stores and can be used as a substitute for Edicol dye. Colours, however, are paler. Food colouring also comes in

paste form which is more intense in colour, but not so easily obtained.

Painting on foil and plastic: mix ½ cup of thick powder paint mixture with 1 teaspoon of dishwashing liquid. If the paint does not adhere, add another ½ teaspoon of dishwashing liquid. The dishwashing liquid makes the paint stick to glossy surfaces.

Powder tempera paint is available in a large variety of colours as a powder and also as a liquid. It is a flat opaque paint which is better suited for some art projects. It covers writing on boxes very well. Put powder in a container, add a little water to make a paste then add a little more to make paint. Liquid starch, cornflour or paper paste can be added to give it transparency and to increase volume as it can be expensive. When dry it may rub off onto hands and clothing. Thick paint sometimes cracks but paper paste added will help prevent this.

Unusual painting tools:
Refillable roll-on deodorant containers filled with paint.
Feather duster used on very large paper as a paint brush.
Plastic squeeze bottles.
Fly swatter.
Dry pine needles tied into a brush.
Paint rollers.
End of a piece of cardboard.

COLLAGE MATERIALS

Crepe paper curls: cut ½cm strips off the end of a roll of crepe paper. Cut through completely one end of strip and roll the strips between your palms to separate the unfolded papers.

How to dye:
Matchsticks, ice block sticks: place in a warm dye mixture. The wood colours more quickly in warm dye. Spread on newspaper to dry.

Paper patty pans: the dye must be tap-water hot to melt the thin waxy film on paper patty pans. Wearing gloves, half-fill empty round 200-gram yoghurt cups with heated dye. Open one pack of paper patty pans. Starting from the bottom (the top ones are smaller), put the bottom group of patty pans into the dye. Poke them down as far as possible. Put in the next batch and push them down, repeat with each batch of paper patty pans until the dye is just covering them. Allow to soak for 24 hours. Pour off the dye and turn yoghurt cups upside down on a tray and drain for several hours. With paper patty pans still in yoghurt cups, turn upright and dry well in the sun or over a heater. This takes one to five days (if they are removed from the containers before they are ready they will not keep their shape). When they feel almost dry, remove them from container so they can dry thoroughly. If paper patty pans take too long to dry, they become mouldy. Cold water dye colours only the rim which gives an unusual effect.

Pasta: wearing gloves, place Edicol (start with ⅛ teaspoon) or food colouring into cold water. Place pasta into the dye, swish it around and remove quickly before it becomes sticky. Spread on a thick wad of newspaper. As it is drying, run your hand over pasta to keep it from adhering to the newspaper.

Dry dye sticks are mentioned in this book (page 9). The brand we used, Di-stix, is available in selected stores throughout Australia.

5

NEIGHBOURHOOD DRAWING (right)

An adult may draw some street crossings on a piece of paper. Each child may then draw in his or her home, playground, trees, cars, shops, neighbourhood playmates and pets. Or drawings may be made on another piece of paper, cut out and stuck on the neighbourhood picture. It's a stimulating way for children to show how they see their own environment.

FINGERPRINT DRAWINGS

Make fingerprints on paper. Draw features on a single print or several fingerprints to make them into quaint creatures, birds, flowers or insects.

6

Picture Show

Picasso has said that adults should not teach children to draw; instead they should be allowed to express their own originality — and we should learn from them. Children have an innate need to express their own interpretation of the world; we can observe much about their view of life from their drawings. For some children it is easier to tell us how they feel by means of crayon and paper, rather than with words.

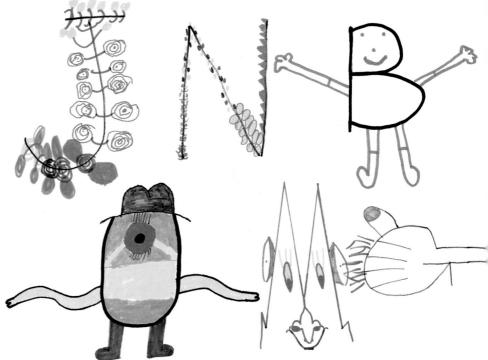

Good quality felt-tipped pens give the greatest colour with good clarity of line. Unfortunately, these pens dry out easily, so must be kept capped. Chalk colours are more vivid if the paper has been dampened with a sponge. They dry with more colour and a slight gloss when the paper has been brushed with evaporated milk or buttermilk before using chalk. Carbon paper is an exciting way for children to make copies of their work. Burnt cork may be used like charcoal. Use long wine corks. An adult should burn the end with a match. A child can draw on paper with the burnt end of the cork. When it wears off, the cork may be burned again. Coloured pencils, wax and chalk crayons and oil pastels are also good drawing tools to use.

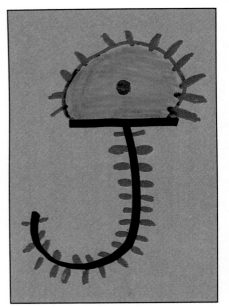

IDEAS TO STIMULATE DRAWING

Children enjoy making drawings from their initials and can produce the most imaginative interpretations. Another idea to inspire individual and original expression is for an adult to scribble on paper and let a young child turn the scribbles into people, animals, space creatures. Turning objects upside down and drawing them provides another interesting perspective. When an everyday object becomes unusual (for example, by turning it upside down) children will more readily try a new interpretation of the object rather than reproducing it accurately.

Fabric designs

YOU WILL NEED:
Dry dye sticks
Fabric (synthetic or a blend of
polyester/cotton, as dry dye
sticks will not work well on pure
cotton, wool or silk)
White drawing paper
Iron
Scissors

1. (Adult) read directions accompanying dry dye sticks carefully.

2. Using dye sticks draw a design or picture on drawing paper. Draw on only one side of paper.

3. (Adult) following directions included in dye sticks packet, transfer drawing from paper to fabric. Cut design out as directed. If you are using a T-shirt or pillowcase, place plain paper inside it to stop dye going through to fabric underneath. Take care not to move paper or a double image will result. Move iron evenly across fabric to prevent steam holes appearing on fabric. If the iron is left in same spot the whole time, colour will not result where steam holes have been sitting on fabric. Unlike other pens which draw directly onto fabric, dry dye sticks allow you to transfer a selected part of a drawing.

Magic drawing

YOU WILL NEED:

Cotton buds
Coloured tissue paper
or white paper painted all
over with Edicol
Liquid bleach
Small bowl or cup
White paper

1. (Adult) put about one table-spoon of bleach in bowl. Replace bleach lid and put it up on shelf out of reach of children.

Place over white or brightly coloured cardboard or paper to make unusual cards or wrapping paper.

2. Put end of cotton bud into bleach and then place that end onto tissue paper and draw a picture. Within a few seconds the area that has been touched with the bleach will turn white. Darker colours may need more bleach. The disappearance of colour on tissue paper shows up better when a sheet of white paper is placed directly underneath.

Crayon etchings

YOU WILL NEED:

Crayons (light colours)
Black crayon or thick black powder paint
Bobby pin or end of paintbrush
Small sheet of paper
Newspaper

1. Pressing firmly, draw a picture all over paper with a thick layer of crayons. Place pad of newspaper under sheet of paper. Cover crayon picture with black crayon or black powder paint. Allow to dry. The newspaper pad helps the black crayon to cover more evenly but it should be removed for the etching, which requires a hard surface.

2. Place paper on one layer of newspaper (to make clean up easier). Make another picture by scraping off black layer of paint or crayon with blunt instrument to reveal colours underneath.

11

Personal book

YOU WILL NEED:

1 metre calico
Shoe laces, wool or
embroidery cotton
Laundry marker or fabric pen
Scissors
Children's favourite drawings
Hole puncher
Clear self-adhesive plastic

1. (Adult) tear or cut calico into equal-sized rectangular shapes. This will be the size of the book.

2. Place rectangular shapes on top of each other. Fold material in half and mark it with sewing pins. Hand sew, with colourful thread, a seam down the centre to hold pages firmly together.

3. Cut out favourite drawings.

4. Cover the drawings with self-adhesive plastic. Punch hole in top of drawings.

5. Attach shoe laces, wool or cotton to book pages by sewing them into place or threading them through two small cuts made in fabric. The drawings may then be tied into book with shoe laces or wool or cotton lengths.

6. Captions may be written on each page. Children can move the drawings around from page to page to suit the story they want to tell.

This is a wonderful way to preserve favourite drawings and to help children learn to tie things.

Leaf rubbings

YOU WILL NEED:

Crayons
Thin paper
Leaves (not too small)
Tape

1. Place leaves on table. Place paper on top of leaves. Tape paper to table to stop it from moving.

2. Remove any paper label from crayon. Place crayon length-ways on paper and rub it back and forth across paper. Tracery of the veins and ridges of the leaves will appear on the paper.
Coins and other textures can also be rubbed in this way.

Colour Our World

Painting is primarily a blend of colour, texture and design. Young children are almost overwhelmed with the sensation of colour blending with colour and are amazed at their own power to create beautiful images, unusual designs and new textures. Paint is thick, drippy, transparent, opaque, airy or glossy. The wonderful qualities of paint combine to lead a child on a new sensory adventure. Encourage the young artist to experiment rather than copy our examples exactly. Mix paints and textures, let different techniques be combined for delightful new effects.

ALL AGES

Easel painting

YOU WILL NEED:

Easel
Large paper
Paint
Long handled paintbrushes
Aprons
Clothes line pegs or tape

1. Put on apron. Clip paper onto easel with clothes line pegs, bulldog clips or tape. Paint pictures onto paper sheets.

2. Remove paper from easel and allow it to dry thoroughly.

The long handled paintbrushes allow more freedom of movement, although shorter handled ones are much easier for younger children. When buying or making an easel, make sure the paint tray has an opening which makes cleaning easier. Sometimes a paint stand is more suitable. Two easels placed next to each other encourages interaction between the children.

Fingerpainting

Fingerpainting is a wonderful sensory experience; children love the feel of paint moving between the fingers. One little girl we know described soap flake fingerpaint (see opposite page) as "so soft and cuddly, I'd like to crawl right into it and go to sleep." Fingerpainting to music can enhance a child's relaxing emotional release.

Some simple preparations will make fingerpainting a pleasant experience for everyone:

1. Aprons must be worn. (Father's old shirt or an old t-shirt will do). Sleeves should be rolled up.

2. Children must stay at the table and keep the paint on the sheet of paper or tabletop if doing a fingerpainting print (see page 40). A bucket of soapy water should be placed next to the table. As soon as fingerpainting is finished, hands should be washed in the soapy water. Children will need help to remove their aprons so that any wet paint from them does not get onto anything else around about. Wipe fingerpaint off the tabletop before it dries and is hard to remove.

3. Paste mixture may be coloured with Edicol dissolved in a little water. Made up powder paint may also be added. For a different colour experience, the children can mix powder paint in powder form into clear fingerpaste. Scented oils (such as oil of cloves or wintergreen) may be added to give a pleasant aroma.

Brown and black fingerpaint are especially helpful to children going through the "dirt" stage. Sand or talcum powder may be added to the fingerpaint to give a different sensory experience. Instant pudding mix makes a wonderful fingerpaint and encourages children who shy away from fingerpaint because it is "too messy".

4. The paper must be heavy enough to withstand the friction and moisture of fingerpainting. Paper must be at least bond weight. If you dampen the tabletop, the paper will not slip. If you have a large roll of paper, try covering the entire tabletop, taping down the edges, and use the large area as a fingerpainting surface.

5. Store fingerpaint in the refrigerator. It should last a week.

Try fingerpainting with wallpaper paste, toothpaste, hand lotion or vaseline or use one of the easy recipes described here.

CORNFLOUR PASTE
YOU WILL NEED:
3 parts water (3 cups)
1 part cornflour (1 cup)
Colouring
Saucepan

1. (Adult) bring water to boil in saucepan. Remove from heat.

2. (Adult) dissolve cornflour in a little cold water and add to hot water, stirring constantly. Boil until clear and thick (about one minute). Add desired colouring.

3. This mixture will be very smooth. Offer it to the children while it is still warm to touch.

4. A tablespoon of glycerine may be added to make it glossy. A ½ cup of soap flakes may be added to give fingerpaint a lumpy texture.

STARCH

YOU WILL NEED:

One part starch granules
(1 cup)
Two parts boiling water (2 cups)
Saucepan
Colouring

1. (Adult) add a small amount of water (about 6 tablespoons) to starch to make a paste.

2. (Adult) add boiling water to starch, stirring constantly. The mixture should become thick and milky glossy. If it doesn't thicken it is because the water isn't hot enough. Simply put it on the stove and bring to the boil. Remove from stove. Add colouring. Add some glycerine and/or ½ cup of soap flakes for a different texture. Give it to children while still warm.

WHIPPED SOAP FLAKES

YOU WILL NEED:

2 cups warm water
1 cup soap flakes
Paint or Edicol
Bowl
Electric mixer
Heavy paper

1. Put water in bowl. (Adult) turn mixer on and add soap flakes. Beat until stiff. Add colouring and mix thoroughly. Remember, this mixture clogs the drain. (See **Note** under Soap Painting, page 30.)

HOMEMADE PASTE

YOU WILL NEED:

1 part water
1 part flour
Colouring
Bowl and spoon

1. Put water into bowl. Add flour, stirring constantly.

2. Add colouring. Salt may be added for a different texture.

Straw painting

YOU WILL NEED:

Food colouring mixed with water or thin paint
Straws
Non-absorbent paper
Spoon or paintbrush

1. Place paper on table. Put a little paint or food colouring on paper with spoon or paintbrush.

2. Point straw in direction you want paint to go, put straw to lips and blow. The paint will fan out to make interesting patterns the more you blow on the straw.

Powder painting

YOU WILL NEED:

Powder paint in small pie tins or bowls
Paintbrushes
Liquid starch
Paper

1. Pour a puddle of starch onto paper. Spread starch over sheet with paintbrush.

2. With another slightly damp paintbrush, pick up the paint powder and dab it onto starch-covered paper. The powder will dissolve and become thick paint — creating a pleasing texture.

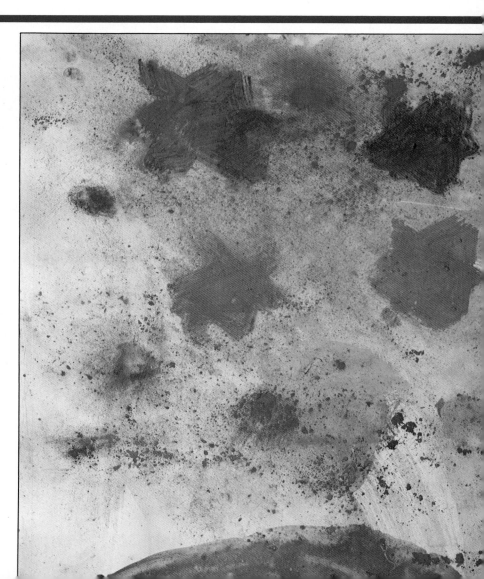

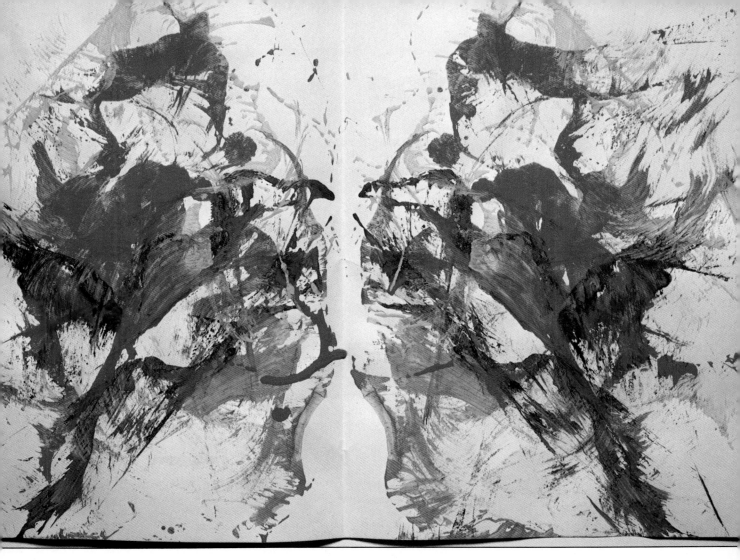

Cord and string painting

YOU WILL NEED:

50cm lengths of string
Paint in polystyrene tray or
shallow dish
Paper folded in half

After gaining a little experience with this method, try using thick and thin paint and mix it with some white glue for a different effect.

1. Place pre-folded piece of paper beside paint tray. Open paper.

2. Drop one end of string into paint, keeping hold of dry end.

3. Pull string out of tray onto paper until paint-covered string is on paper and dry end of the string is at the edge of paper.

4. While still holding onto the string, fold paper on top of the string with free hand.

5. Press down on paper and pull string out. Open paper.

6. Repeat with a new colour. Use separate strings for each colour.

7. For a different design, drag string sideways around the paper while pulling it out.

Body painting

YOU WILL NEED:

Sheet of paper, larger
than the child
Crayons
Paint
Paintbrushes
Scissors

1. Place paper on floor. Child should lie face up on top of paper.

2. Draw an outline around child's whole body.

3. Colour in body drawn on paper with crayons or paint. Older children may do a series of characters.

4. Finished figures may be cut out and used for further play. This activity encourages development of a positive self-image.

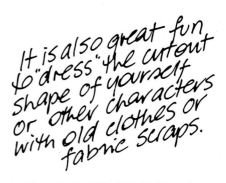

It is also great fun to "dress" the cutout shape of yourself or other characters with old clothes or fabric scraps.

Bubble painting

YOU WILL NEED:
Dishwashing liquid
Powder paint or Edicol
Straws
Paper
Empty yoghurt container

1. Pour ¼ cup of dishwashing liquid into container. Mix a small amount of water with powder paint.

2. Add paint mixture to dishwashing liquid until colour is intense.

3. Practise blowing on a straw.

4. Put straw into paint mixture and blow until the bubbles slightly overflow the container.

5. Roll paper around gently on top of bubbles so as not to burst the bubbles. Try not to press paper flat on top of bubbles. Repeat the process with several colours for a pretty sheet of multi-coloured paper. Allow to dry before using.

Blot painting

YOU WILL NEED:

Paint
Paper
Spoon or paintbrush

1. Fold paper in half. Open it. Very young children will need the paper to be pre-folded.

2. Spoon or brush paint out in drops onto paper, mainly along the central fold line.

3. Refold and rub with palm of hand from fold out to edge of paper. Open out and admire the effect.

Cut the butterfly out and hang it on your wall as a kite-like decoration.

Try using your feet!

YOU WILL NEED:

Powder paint
Large baking dish
Long piece of paper, about
2 metres long and as heavy
as possible
Bucket of water and soap
Towel
Rocks

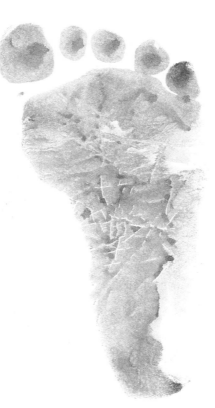

1. Cover bottom of baking dish with thin layer of paint.

2. Lay paper down on grass. Weigh down its edges with rocks or similar heavy items to stop wind blowing paper up. Place baking dish at one end of paper. Place bucket of water at other end of paper.

3. Place bare feet in paint in baking dish then walk along paper. Make any pattern with your feet. After reaching the other end, step in bucket of water and wash feet clean with soap. Dry with towel.

4. Change colour in baking dish and repeat. Get a new piece of paper before painting becomes too wet and slippery. Hold a friend's hand.

Note: If only lightweight paper is available or if paper tears when it is trodden on because grass underneath is uneven, place paper on a concrete path. Try footpainting with gumboots.

Window painting

YOU WILL NEED:

Paintbrushes
Newspapers
Tape
Powder paint (this wipes off windows easiest and has the most intense colours. Soap paint and any paint mixed with white liquid shoe polish is also suitable. Paste and starch-based paint is hard to wash off the windows)

1. Tape newspaper to bottom of window to protect floor and ledges.

2. Paint onto inside of window as rain will wash off any outside painting. Paintings can be left for days or weeks. Wash off with sponge and soapy water. The paint does not mark window in any way but the longer it is left, the harder it is to remove as it seems to bake on.

Some window paintings are so pretty you'll wish they'd last forever!

Crayon-resist painting

YOU WILL NEED:
Crayons
Thin powder paint or Edicol
Paper
Paintbrush

1. Draw a heavy design on paper with crayons.

2. Cover drawing with paint. Best results occur when light coloured crayons are used with dark paint or dark coloured crayons are used with light paint.
Thin powder paint (not ready made) gives the most dramatic result because of its opaque quality.

Marble painting

YOU WILL NEED:
Marbles
Paint in bowls
Straining spoon
Shoe box or similar box
Paper
Bowl of clear water

1. Place marbles in paint bowls containing various colours. Place sheet of paper in bottom of box.

2. Spoon several different coloured marbles into the box. Roll them around so they leave a coloured pattern on the paper. Take marbles out with spoon and wash them in bowl of clear water. Repeat with different coloured marbles. Take paper out of box and dry.

Wall hanging

YOU WILL NEED:

Bright, solid coloured fabric in a
rectangular shape
Powder paint
Paintbrushes
Two sticks, each a little longer
than the width of the cloth
Thin wool, threaded through a
darning needle
String, a little longer than
one stick
Two thumb tacks

1. (Adult) press fabric with iron to
remove creases.

2. Place fabric right side down on
table. Place stick at top, about 4cm
down from top edge. Fold fabric
over stick. Straight stitch to secure
fabric around stick. Repeat at bottom of fabric. Turn fabric over.

3. Paint picture on fabric. (Sticks
may be temporarily removed.)

4. Attach string to each end of top
stick with thumb tacks. For example, push a thumb tack part way
into centre of each end of stick. Tie
off each end of string around
thumb tack and push thumb tacks
all the way into stick. Staples or
glue can also be used.

Note: Younger children will need
help with steps 2 and 4.

Paper Dyeing

YOU WILL NEED:

Rice paper sheet from
newsagent, coffee filter paper,
blotting paper or paper towels
Food colouring in several bowls
Eye droppers

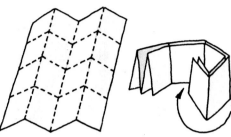

1. Fold paper sheet into eighths or sixteenths.

2. Dip one corner of paper into one colour and remove.

3. Dip another corner of paper into another colour and remove.

4. Repeat with all corners of paper. Unfold and dry. Unusual folds make more interesting pictures. Snowflakes (page 121) look beautiful if they are folded and dipped.

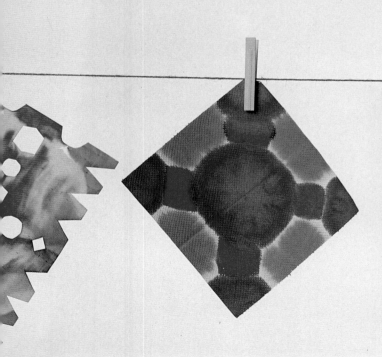

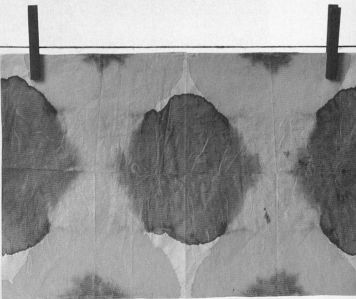

For variation, use eye droppers to create a colourful design on the paper. Fill eye dropper with colour from one bowl and drop a spot of colour onto the paper. Use another eye dropper to add another colour. The colours will blend to make a pattern. It is a good idea for the child to work at a table. Absorbent paper will give the best results.

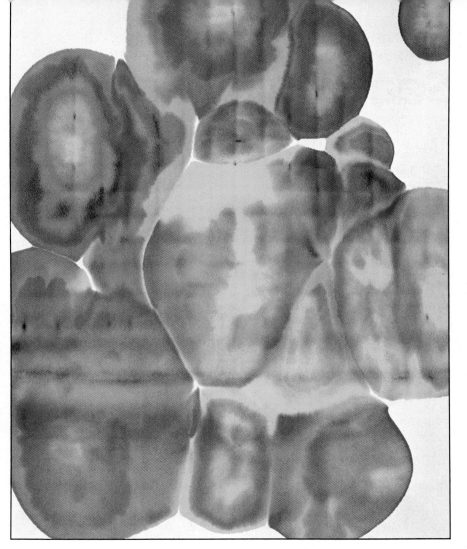

Soap painting

YOU WILL NEED:

1 cup soap flakes
Mixing bowl
½ cup cold water
Electric mixer
Containers
Paint or Edicol
Large paintbrushes
Heavy paper

1. Put cold water in bowl. (Adult) turn mixer on and add soap flakes, while beating, until mixture is the consistency of stiff egg whites.

2. Add colour or use white mixture on coloured paper.

Note: This paint dries with a three dimensional effect. Coloured sand or glitter will stick to soap paint — no glue needed. Dispose of soap mixture in rubbish bin as it will clog the drain. This mixture looks good enough to eat and young children will need to be reminded that it is not food. The consistency of soap mixtures vary with the temperature of the water and the amount of flakes used. As long as they are beaten enough, all batches are useful for art work.

Soap snow

YOU WILL NEED:

2 cups soap flakes
½ cup cold water
Cardboard or heavy paper
Piping bag
Paint or Edicol
Electric mixer
Mixing bowl and smaller bowl

1. Put cold water into bowl. (Adult) turn mixer on and add soap flakes. Beat until stiff. Do not underbeat.

2. Put a portion of soap snow into a smaller bowl, add colouring and beat thoroughly.

3. Put into piping bag and pipe onto paper. Repeat with another colour. Soap snow dries to a fluffy, fragile texture. Remember, this mixture clogs the drain (see **Note,** left).

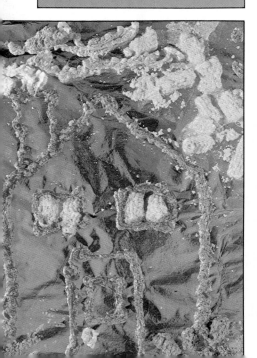

Squeeze bottle painting

YOU WILL NEED:

Flour
Salt
Paint
Heavy paper or cardboard
Plastic squeeze bottles

1. (Adult) mix equal parts of flour and salt. Add paint to form a paste. Pour into plastic squeeze bottles.

2. Squeeze paint onto heavy paper. Salt gives the designs a glistening quality when dry.

While painting is still wet, sprinkle glitter over the paint to give it a real sparkle.

Mural painting

A mural is a very large painting on a wall. It is best done outside by clipping, stapling or taping a long piece of paper to a fence and allowing children to paint on the paper. Several children can enjoy painting on the same piece of paper. An end roll of heavy weight paper — one or more metres wide — is often available, free of charge, from newspaper publishers or printers. Mural painting is a fun group activity especially at children's parties.

Make up your own play and use mural as backdrop (scenery). Cut into sections, tape to a wall and change it each time for different sets.

Weaving trays

YOU WILL NEED:

Polystyrene packing trays
Knife
Wool threaded through a darning needle
Wool, ribbon, long reeds or grass for weaving
Sea shells or gum nuts

1. (Adult) cut a geometric section in centre of tray and remove it; a square is easiest for a beginner.

2. Tie knot in end of wool on needle. Put threaded needle through tray, about 3cm in from edge of cutout shape. Pull thread across to other side and bring needle up through tray. Repeat this process back and forth across cutout section to make warp strings. Strings strung in one direction only (e.g. left to right) tend to make square or rectangular weaves whereas wool strung in all directions across cutout shape enables unusual circles to be woven.

3. Weave ribbon or double thread of wool back and forth in a straight line or weave one or more circles depending on design of warp strings. To keep weaving square, push needle through side of tray after completing a line then continue weaving. Sea shells or gum nuts can be strung onto wool during weaving. Long reeds or grasses may also be used in place of ribbon or wool.

Younger children need supervision until they have had a little practice. Trays can be used as place mats or wall hangings, or the ends of the warp strings can be cut from tray and, tied together two at a time (to stop weaving from coming undone), used as pot holders.

When threading, the end of the string must be stiff so children can push it through a hole easily. This can be done by either wrapping a piece of sticky tape around the end of the string or by dunking the end in melted wax and leaving it to set. String, twine, wool and ribbon are all suitable for threading.

Alternatively, string may be put through a bodkin or darning needle which is safe and easy for a child to control.

Any object with a hole in it can be used for threading. Coloured macaroni and pasta shapes, cereals, cut straws, cotton reels, buttons or even paper with holes punched in it make excellent threading materials. Gum nuts are interesting but holes have to be drilled to allow threading.

Fabric to be used by children for sewing must be loosely woven so it is easy for them to get a blunt needle through; burlap or netting is a good choice. Fabric is easier to handle if it is thumbtacked onto a simple wooden frame.

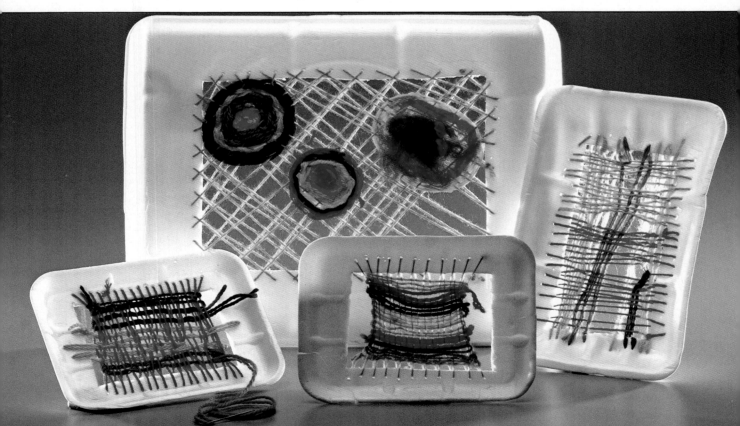

String and Things

Children can create wonderfully imaginative articles when sewing, threading or weaving. The actions involved help their small muscle development and control, as well as hand-eye co-ordination. When weaving, the interlocking threads give new and intriguing textural effects that children can explore with their fingers. Easy weaving projects give them confidence in their new-found skill; they are encouraged to try difficult tapestries and other weaving projects as they grow older.

String balloons

YOU WILL NEED:

About 20 pieces of colourful wool or cotton string, about 60 cm in length
Thick, sturdy balloon
Extra strong liquid starch (see pages 4-5)

1. Blow up balloon and tie a double knot in end of it.

2. Dip a string in starch mixture, making sure it is completely covered with starch but not too heavy to hang on balloon. Wrap starched strings around balloon one by one making sure both ends of string are securely plastered down. The balloon should be fairly well covered with string but not completely covered so that string slips off. Allow balloon and string to dry overnight. Pop balloon and remove it when thoroughly dry.
Delicate lacy balloons can be made with cotton on a small balloon.
Tissue paper may be added on top of the starched wool or cotton to give a different effect.

OVER 3 YEARS

Basket stitching

YOU WILL NEED:

Loosely woven small cane baskets
Colourful wool or other material threaded through a bodkin

Stitch desired pattern through holes in basket. The firmness of the basket makes it easy for youngsters to hold it and push the bodkin through the woven surface.
Older children have a longer attention span and may be interested in stitching on larger baskets.

Branch weaving

YOU WILL NEED:

Branch with at least three smaller branches shooting out from it

Coloured wool, about 2 metres in length

Nature items (long grasses, feathers, sea shells, corn husks, seed pods)

1. Starting at the top or bottom of one small branch, loop wool around a branch to secure it. Continue to next small branch. Wrap wool around smaller branches to make a warp base moving up or down branches, depending on where weaving began. Warp threads are the first threads on the frame. They are stretched lengthwise and usually placed side by side on the frame.

2. Weave wool, grasses and other intriguingly shaped nature items through warp wool strands. Alternatively, some children will prefer to wrap wool around branches in a random manner.

Children 3½ to 5 years old made this wonderful woven wall hanging (left). They used a U-shaped branch, tied wool from one side to the other, tying off a knot each time. Each thread was about 3cm from the next. Then they all had fun threading through, under and over, interesting materials such as feathers, leaves, wild grasses, bamboo and strips of leather from Reverse Garbage in Sydney which supplies excess materials from industry. Adults may be able to locate similar organisations in each major city.

Sewing cards for beginners

YOU WILL NEED:
Cardboard
Clear self-adhesive plastic
Hole puncher
Children's drawings
Wool, threaded through a
bodkin if desired
Scissors
Pen

1. (Adult) cut cardboard into desired shape. Children can draw on cardboard if they choose.

2. (Adult) punch holes along edge of shape and as far into centre of cardboard as possible.

3. Sew or thread wool through holes. Buttons, macaroni, or cut straws may be added to wool while threading through holes.

For variation, cover a child's drawing or magazine cutout on both sides with self-adhesive plastic. (Adult) cut shape out and punch holes through it. Thread wool through holes.

Necklaces & bracelets

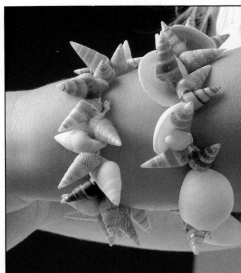

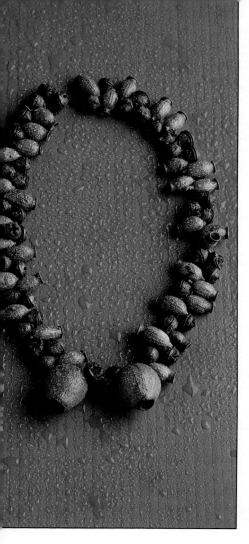

Shell wind chime

YOU WILL NEED:
Sea shells
Strong coloured wool
Electric drill with steel bit
Scissors
Branch or driftwood

Make wind chimes too from hollow dried bamboo sections, or metal bottle tops.

1. (Adult) drill hole in one end of each sea shell.

2. Cut wool appropriate length to tie to each end of branch so that it may be looped and hung up.

3. (Adult) hang up the branch so that it is at child's working level.

4. Cut a length of wool at least 50cm long. Tie it to the branch. Thread a sea shell onto the other end. Push shell close to the branch, tie a double knot to hold in place. Repeat with other shells, leaving space between. An adult may need to hold shells while the child ties them into place.

5. Thread and knot shells into other parts of branch. Take care not to make one side heavier than the other. Try to tie shells close enough to touch shells on other strings when the wind blows.

YOU WILL NEED:
Macaroni, sea shells, gum nuts, buttons and so on
Beads out of jewellery modelling mixture (see page 66)
Wool, embroidery thread, ribbon on bodkin, if desired
Elastic thread

1. (Adult) tie first item to be threaded onto end of string to prevent other items slipping off.

2. Thread items onto string to make an interesting pattern.

Long necklaces can be joined in a knot. Bracelets must be threaded onto elastic thread so they will stretch over a hand. Short necklaces can be put on elastic thread or a hook and eye can be used as a clasp. A necklace may also be tied around the neck each time it is worn. Tie a large knot at each end of the wool or thread to stop items from slipping off.

Fingerpainting print

YOU WILL NEED:

Table top — preferably made of
plastic laminate
Fingerpaint
Paper
Bucket of warm soapy water
Towel
Apron

1. Put a small puddle of fingerpaint
onto table top.

2. Put on an apron. Fingerpaint on
table top. When finished, wash
hands in bucket of soapy water and
dry them thoroughly.

3. Place a large sheet of paper on
top of the fingerpainting. Rub back
of paper all over with clean, dry
hands. Slowly lift paper off table
and hang it up to dry.

Prints can also be made of pictures
painted on the table top.

Making a Great Impression

A print is making an impression of an object onto paper or another surface. Printing encourages an appreciation of texture and the development of design through the repetition of an impression. Children are also fascinated by the pattern reversal that occurs with printmaking. Because small muscle co-ordination is not necessary to quickly achieve attractive reproductions of objects, young children experience a sense of great accomplishment.

PRINTING TECHNIQUES

Paint is applied to the object to be printed usually by three methods: painting with a brush, rolling over the object with a hard paint roller or print roller that has been covered with paint by rolling in a paint-filled tray, or by pressing it on a print pad.

To make a print pad: Place a thin sponge into a polystyrene tray or small bowl. Place several spoonsful of paint onto the sponge. This helps the object to collect a minimal amount of paint to avoid smearing the print. Make a cushion by placing a newspaper under the paper on which the print impression is to be made.

Leaf printing

YOU WILL NEED:

Cardboard
Leaves
P.V.A. glue
Powder paint
Print roller
Absorbent paper
Spoon

1. Arrange leaves in desired design onto cardboard. Glue leaves onto cardboard and allow to dry.

2. Put a spoonful of paint onto a flat surface (e.g cardboard). Move print roller through paint until it is evenly coated. Roll paint onto the leaves (a brush will not work).

3. Lay a piece of paper on top of the leaves. Rub the paper with a clean, dry hand. The raised veins and edges will make an impressive design. Take several prints from the same painting. The same technique can be used with wire mesh, lace or netting instead of leaves.

Clay printing

YOU WILL NEED:

Tools (pencils, nails, bottle caps, pieces of wire screen, biscuit cutters, cooking utensils, shower nozzles)
Earth clay or play dough
Print pad (see previous page)
Paper

1. Roll clay or play dough into ball. Flatten it until it is about 4cm thick.

2. On one side of clay, press any tools in to make a design. You can also draw on the clay with a thick nail or the end of a paintbrush.

3. Gently press clay onto print pad, remove, press onto paper. Repeat with different colours and designs.

Spatter stencil

YOU WILL NEED:

Old toothbrush
Comb or piece of wire screen
taped to an old picture frame
or a box screen
Thin powder paint in a bowl
or thin Edicol
Paper
Pressed leaves, flowers or
any flat items
Large cardboard box
Tape

Try the spatter technique using chalk scraped over screen above glue or starch-covered paper.

1. If working in a restricted space, or in the house where furniture may get damaged, get a large grocery box and cut out one side. Place sheet of paper inside box and tape edges down so that it will not shift.

2. Lay leaves, flowers, grasses on paper; or cut stencils from cardboard or other suitable material.

3. Place piece of wire screen about 10cm above level of paper or hold comb about this height above paper. Our photograph is of a box screen made for preschool or kindergarten use. It is easy to improvise with an old picture frame.

4. Dip toothbrush into paint.

5. Draw the paint-filled brush many times across the flat side of the comb or across the screen. If the brush is loaded with paint, spatter drops will be big and coarse.

6. Allow paint to dry, then remove leaves and other decoration.

Fish printing

YOU WILL NEED:

Fresh dead fish with large scales (flat if possible)
Powder paint
Paintbrush
Newspaper
Absorbent paper (blotting paper works well)

1. Lay fish on newspaper. Dry if still damp. Paint side of fish.

2. Carefully place absorbent paper on fish. With flat, dry hand, rub paper all over painted fish. Lift paper off and allow to dry. Several prints may be taken each time the fish is painted. Sometimes the first print is not always successful as there is too much paint on the fish. After thorough cleansing, the fish is still perfectly good to eat.

Do coloured prints of small fish or prawns, cut them out and add them to the play aquarium. (page 82)

Sponge printing

YOU WILL NEED:
Small thick sponges
Clothes pegs
Print pads with different coloured paint
Paper
Scissors

1. (Adult) cut sponges into various shapes. Cut two slots in top of sponge, about 1cm deep and 2cm apart, for peg to clip into. Clip clothes peg to top of sponge to act as a handle. Two thin sponges can be glued together with P.V.A glue and used in same way.

2. Press sponge onto the printing pad, remove, stamp it onto paper. Repeat this process with different shapes and colours. This has a very interesting textural effect.

Fruit, vegetable and gadget printing

YOU WILL NEED:

Oranges, lemons, potatoes, carrots, onions, potato mashers, keys, buttons, Lego blocks or any flat objects
Print pad
Paper
Knife

1. (Adult) cut fruit and vegetables in half to make a flat surface. Sometimes a fruit or vegetable must be allowed to drain upside down on a paper towel before it is able to absorb paint from the pad.

2. Press printing object into print pad, remove, press onto paper. Repeat with different colours and fruit, vegetables or gadgets.
Hand prints can also be made by pressing hand onto print pad and then onto paper. Children over five may be able to cut a pattern into a potato with plastic knife, spoon or melon scoop to get an unusual print on paper.

Marbling

YOU WILL NEED:
Waterproof ink, various colours
Large polystyrene trays
Plastic spoons
Light-coloured blotting paper

1. Put on an apron.

2. Half-fill trays with water and gently drop small amounts of ink onto surface of water. Stir mixture very carefully and slowly.

Note: For more intense and distinct colours, substitute the waterproof ink with the following powder paint mixture: 2 tablespoons powder paint mixed in a disposable container with 2 tablespoons of cooking oil (instead of water) and one tablespoon of mineral turpentine (N.B. poisonous). A little more care must be taken in cleaning up because of the oil. The prints take several days to dry.

3. The ink will float, swirl and ooze to form fascinating patterns.

4. Place paper on top of floating colours for 30 seconds. Quickly lift off, turn over, and immediately hold horizontally to stop paint running. Allow to dry on flat surface.

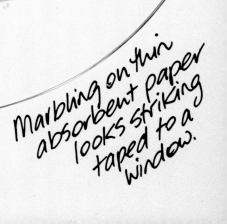

Marbling on thin absorbent paper looks striking taped to a window.

String block printing

YOU WILL NEED:
String or rope
Small blocks of wood
Powder paint in about 1cm
deep shallow dish
Paintbrushes
Paper

1. Wrap string around wooden block several times (making sure there is not a build up of string in one spot), and tie it in place.

2. Place paint in shallow dish. Press string block into paint so string picks up colour. Alternatively, paint string with paintbrush.

3. Make a print by placing string block on paper and pressing. Move block around in different directions until an interesting print design is obtained.

Sticking Together

Pictured: Evocative wall collage using cut-up finger paintings for trees, patty pan loops and rolled-up newspaper for birds' nests.

Collage is an exciting
technique of pasting, gluing, taping,
stapling paper, fabrics, dried food,
feathers, nuts and other objects onto a
surface. The tactile nature of building and
creating with various collage materials can
be fascinating for children. It is exciting
for them to make something that can be
both felt and seen — "a feeling picture".

Note: The choice of adhesive is important if the collage creation is not to become unstuck. Homemade (see pages 4-5) and commercial pastes are suitable but may soon crack or peel off. Use P.V.A. glue and high quality wallpaper paste if collage is to be kept. Apply glue or paste with brushes, ice block sticks or similar objects — it's highly frustrating to have fingers behave like fly paper, attracting all the bits and pieces you're trying to stick together. P.V.A. glue will hold together cardboard, paper, fabric, wood, seed pods and other light or medium-weight collage materials. It is not successful with most metals, glass and a few plastics. The glue is easiest to control from a squirt bottle which can be refilled from a larger bottle of glue. P.V.A. glue dries to a colourless finish in a few hours. Refer to glossary for instructions on preparing collage materials.

Assorted collage materials—including dyed pasta, pipe cleaners, cellophane, magazine pages, crepe paper—can be collected together, as above.

52

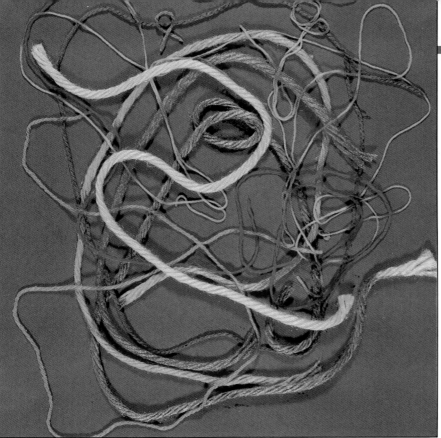

String collage

YOU WILL NEED:
Colourful string or wool
Paper paste or liquid starch
Heavy paper
Polystyrene tray
Scissors

1. Cut string or wool into 30cm lengths. Soak for a few minutes in tray of paste or starch.

2. Place polystyrene tray along top edge of paper. Pull one paste-covered strand out of the tray and arrange it on paper into desired design. Repeat with different coloured string or wool.

Add string or cooked pasta to a starch or paste-based fingerpainting and move items around to form a design.

OVER 4 YEARS

Paper dolls

YOU WILL NEED:
Doll shapes drawn onto
heavy paper
P.V.A. glue
Crayons
Wool, fabric scraps, buttons
Scissors

1. Cut various doll shapes.

2. Colour dolls with crayons. Older children may draw faces on dolls.

3. Glue wool, buttons and fabric scraps onto doll to dress it.

Nature collage

YOU WILL NEED:

Heavy paper or paper plates
P.V.A. glue
Leaves, nuts, pine needles,
pebbles, bark

1. Put a little puddle of glue on paper or paper plate.

2. Place leaves, nuts, pebbles and other items on glue. Allow collage to dry overnight.

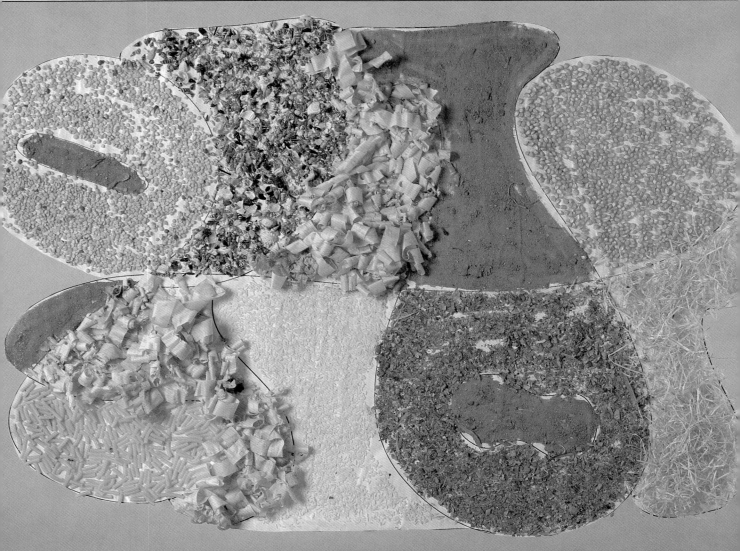

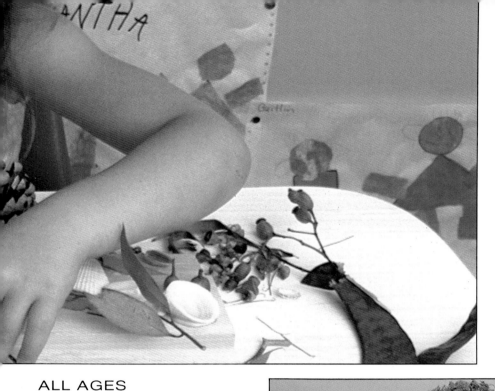

Wood collage

YOU WILL NEED:
Wood scraps, all shapes and sizes
Wood shavings
P.V.A. glue
Cardboard, if desired

1. Stick a variety of wood scraps or shavings together with glue, or glue them onto cardboard.

2. When glue is dry the wood scraps can be painted.

Abstract collage

YOU WILL NEED:
Macaroni
Spaghetti
Beans
Seeds
Cereals
Sand
Shells
P.V.A. glue
Heavy paper or paper plates, boxes or cans

1. Cover small area of paper or item to be decorated with glue.

2. Stick on macaroni, spaghetti, beans, seeds and cereals.

3. Repeat steps 1 and 2 until remainder of item is covered with the collage materials.

For variation, draw a design on paper and fill in the shapes with different collage materials.

Other puppet ideas: round or wriggly balloons, decorated cardboard boxes or tubes.

Fun on a

YOU WILL NEED:

Cardboard
P.V.A. glue
Ice block sticks
Tape
Children's drawings

Puppet Play

Puppetry is a land of magic for children, a chance for make-believe and self-expression. Creativity is encouraged through the variety of puppets to make, from stick people figures to finger puppets and quirky creatures made from socks, wooden spoons, paper boxes and tubes or pine cones, gum nuts and Banksias. Children learn to communicate through puppet play: they interact and lose inhibitions by communicating their own views of life situations.

stick

1. Glue drawings onto cardboard. Drawing around a hand makes an interesting shape for a child to make into a creature.

2. (Adult) cut out drawing. Tape ice block stick to the back of the cardboard. This becomes the handle with which to hold and play-act with the puppet.

Finger puppets

YOU WILL NEED:

Felt, about 9cm x 8cm
Sewing machine
Fabric scraps, buttons,
sequins, feathers
P.V.A., clear craft or hobby glue
suitable for fabric
Scissors

1. (Adult) cut two pieces of felt, about 6cm long and 4cm wide.

2. (Adult) place one piece of felt on top of other. Sew a zig zag stitch around the felt, making the top rounded and leaving the bottom open for finger access.

3. Glue or sew on any materials to create an animal or person.

PAPER FINGER PUPPETS

YOU WILL NEED:

Coloured cardboard
Felt-tipped pens
Paint
Collage materials
Tape
P.V.A. glue
Scissors

1. Draw face or animal shape onto cardboard, about 8cm long and 5cm wide. Cut out shape.

2. (Adult) cut a rectangular strip of cardboard long enough to wind around child's finger.

3. Glue or tape ends of strip together to make a circle.

4. Glue back of cutout drawing onto cardboard circle.

5. Decorate puppet with paper, feathers or other collage materials.

Wooden spoons

YOU WILL NEED:

Wooden spoons
Paint (powder paint is more distinctive)
Paintbrushes
Felt-tipped pens
Wool or cotton wool
Fabric scraps
P.V.A. glue

1. Paint wooden spoon white or light colour.

2. Glue wool strands or cotton wool on spoon for hair. If using wool strands it is easier to glue wool around edge of spoon and across top and then add another layer running from front to back.

3. Paint face onto spoon. Inside or outside surfaces are both suitable.

4. Wrap fabric around handle. Secure with glue.
For variation, use crepe paper, tissue paper or aluminium foil to cover handle.

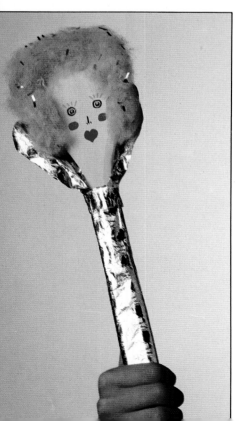

Nature puppets

YOU WILL NEED:
Pine cones, coconut fibre, gum nuts, moss, leaves, seed-boxes of the Banksia tree or the horned seed pod of the Honey Flower (which makes Mountain Devil puppets)

1. Glue or tie stick or branch to appropriate cone or seed-box for head or face of puppet.

2. Glue moss, coconut fibre, leaves or similar materials for hair.

OVER 3 YEARS

Socks

YOU WILL NEED:
Socks
Felt, ribbon, wool and fabric scraps
Buttons
Feathers, sequins
P.V.A., clear craft or hobby glue suitable for fabric
Darning needles threaded with wool (children over six may be able to use large standard sewing needles)

1. Put hand inside sock to prevent sewing or gluing both sides of sock together.

2. Glue or sew on any of the materials to create an animal or person out of the sock. Plastic eyes or buttons are excellent for eyes.

Hand puppets and more

YOU WILL NEED:

Fabric
Sewing machine or large
needle and heavy thread
Laundry markers, felt-tipped
pens or fabric markers (read
directions enclosed).

1. Place hand on fabric, spread
fingers out and draw around hand
with marker.

2. (Adult) cut two pieces of fabric
about 2cm outside the outline,
leaving a wide wrist for the hand to
slip into the puppet. Stitch around
the outside of the puppet with sewing machine, leaving the wrist
open. Alternatively the child may
be able to stitch around the outside of the puppet shape, with a
large needle in running stitch.

For variation, glue on coloured
wool, fabric scraps and other materials for animal features. Stitch or
glue fabric pieces together.

STICK FIGURE PUPPETS

YOU WILL NEED:

Ice block sticks
Paint
Paintbrushes
Pen

1. Paint a number of ice block
sticks white or any pale colour. It is
harder to paint features on dark
coloured sticks.

2. Paint or draw faces onto sticks.
Make a whole family of colourful
stick figure puppets.

'WALKING' PUPPETS

YOU WILL NEED:

Children's drawings
Scissors
Cardboard
P.V.A. glue

1. Glue the drawing onto a piece of
stiff paper or cardboard.

2. (Adult) cut out the drawing, leaving a base at least 8cm deep. Cut
two holes about 1cm apart in the
bottom of the drawing large
enough to slip two fingers through.

3. Put two fingers through the
holes in the puppet. The fingers
become the puppet's legs.

Play dough

COOKED SALT DOUGH

YOU WILL NEED:

1 cup salt
2 cups flour
4 teaspoons cream of tartar
2 tablespoons cooking oil
2 cups water
Powder paint or Edicol
Saucepan

Method: Mix ingredients in saucepan. Add colouring. (Adult) cook on medium heat for three to five minutes, stirring constantly until it becomes stiff. Store in airtight container in refrigerator. It will last for quite a while and has the consistency of commercially prepared play dough. Additional colour may be worked into dough.

UNCOOKED SALT DOUGH

This is the easiest recipe; it can be made in less than three minutes. Let children make it themselves whenever possible.

YOU WILL NEED:

2 cups flour
1 cup salt
1 tablespoon cooking oil
1 cup water
Powder paint or food colouring
Bowl
Spoons

Method: Mix powder paint with flour and salt (food colouring may be added to water as an alternative). Add oil and water. Knead. Children will like to use rollers, biscuit cutters and toothpicks with dough. Store dough in plastic bags. If it becomes sticky, add more flour. Dough will keep for more than a week, even longer if it's kept in a refrigerator but it has a tendency to crumble. Small shapes of this mixture can be baked in a 350° oven for 45 minutes to make them hard.
Makes enough for six children.

Children will sometimes want to add more flour to play dough to make it seem like they are really bakers. Occasionally, leave the dough white so they can colour it themselves with powder paint in plastic salt shakers. Fragrances may be added to any of the doughs. Let children mix different coloured dough together; this will give a marbled effect. Wash off utensils used to make dough before it dries on them. Play dough will clog the drain so don't try to dispose of it by washing it away. Disinfectants and alum are sometimes added as preservatives but they are not necessary in recipes with a high salt content. Salt sometimes attracts moisture if dough is in a sealed container, so if the mixture is sticky, just add a little flour to get the right consistency.

Among the infinite number of play dough things to make is the birthday 'cake' pictured above.

Children love holding soft, pliable materials in their hands and squeezing them to make shapes; they pound, poke, pull, roll, twist and knead. Dough and clay give children the opportunity to demonstrate their ideas and to experience the delight of moulding something and then reshaping it into another new creation. Older children sometimes make balls, pies, biscuits, snakes, birthday cakes and a variety of animals and people from dough. Earth clay responds more to a child's touch than dough — a little water added to its surface makes it more flexible.

Nice Touch

Beads to wear

YOU WILL NEED:

¾ cup flour
½ cup cornflour
½ cup salt
Powder paint or Edicol (if colour is desired)
⅜ cup warm water
Bowl
Toothpicks

Note: All play dough recipes may be used for jewellery, however those recipes made with salt tend to have a white residue which is particularly noticeable on dark coloured play dough.

Method: Mix all ingredients in bowl. Add warm water gradually until mixture can be kneaded into a stiff dough. Dust with dry flour to reduce stickiness. Mixture may be rolled into balls for beads. Pierce each bead with toothpick or large blunt needle and allow to dry for a few days. Large beads take longer to dry. Holes should be checked after a day to see if they need re-punching. Paint if desired. This recipe makes a reasonably smooth dough that retains most of its colour when dry. The beads may be coated with clear gloss enamel to bring out the colour.

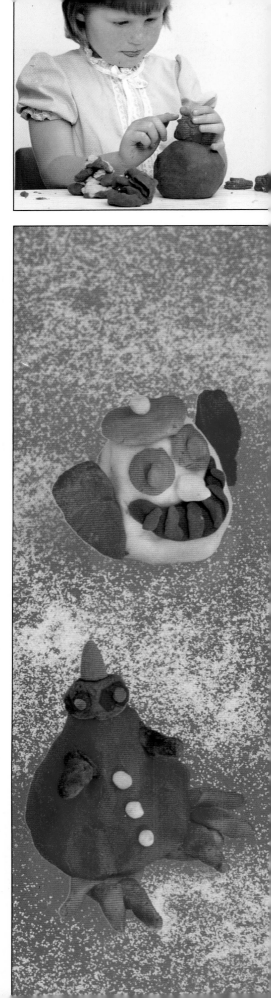

Play dough creatures

YOU WILL NEED:

Different coloured play dough
(how to make, page 64)
Plastic eyes or buttons
Pipe cleaners

Children delight in moulding colourful dough into unusual creatures that show off their imagination and creative thinking. They can roll or pound play dough into fat round shapes, long thin sausage shapes or odd geometric shapes.

Different coloured play dough or stick-on plastic eyes, buttons or pipe cleaners can be added for features. There's no end to the fantastic creations a child's imagination can produce from supple play dough.

Try earth clay

Earth clay is available at craft shops and art supply stores, but buy it in solid form as it is messy to make up from powder. One kilo packages are usually available. Pieces of clay can be sliced off this hunk easily with a string tied to two empty thread reels. Interesting textures can be made by scraping or pressing objects into the clay. Children may want to save the clay objects they have moulded. Let the objects dry thoroughly and they can be painted or lacquered and glued onto a wooden base if desired. It is not advisable to fire the clay products of young children as any air bubbles trapped in the clay will explode and someone will be very disappointed. Earth clay is a bit messy. The table top can be protected with a heavy garbage bag that has been cut open and taped down. This or any similar material can be thrown out afterwards. Save all excess clay in an airtight container to prevent it drying out. If storing for more than a few days, press a thumb into each clay ball and fill hole with water. Clay can clog drains so scrape the excess into storage container. Although the main purpose of clay is manual manipulation, every child should experience the delight of putting it through a garlic press.

CLAY WIND CHIME

YOU WILL NEED:

Earth clay
Spatula
Rolling pin
Tools such as nails, biscuit cutters, garlic press, knives
Fishing line
Coat hanger or branch
Ceramic kiln

1. Roll out a small portion of earth clay 1cm to 2cm thick. Cut desired shape out of flat clay. Using the tools, gently press texture marks into clay shape and attach additional pieces of clay. Make a hole in the top and bottom for hanging. Put spatula under shape and move it to a place to dry. Make a dozen or more different shapes for wind chimes.

2. (Adult) when thoroughly dry take the shapes to a school or craft shop kiln to be bisque fired. This gives them the ringing quality of wind chimes.

3. (Adult) tie short pieces of fishing line through the holes in the chimes. About four knots need to be made in fishing line to keep it in place. Tie three or four chimes together in a row to make a string of chimes. Tie strings of chimes to a branch or coat hanger. The fishing line gives the chimes a better tone, but wool may be used.

PAPERWEIGHT

YOU WILL NEED:

Earth clay
Paint (powder paint is suitable)

1. Make the fish (left) or any shape desired out of earth clay. Flatten the bottom and allow to dry.

2. Paint designs onto the clay. (Adult) when dry, paint clay with clear gloss enamel or lacquer. Rocks can also be painted, lacquered, and used as paperweights.

Box sculpture

YOU WILL NEED:

Cardboard boxes, all shapes and sizes
Cardboard tubes
Powder paint (this covers writing on boxes well)
Tape
P.V.A. glue
Heavy wool or string
Collage materials

1. Tape boxes and tubes together to make space-age cities, trains, animals or abstract sculptures.

2. Paint cardboard sculpture. Glue on any collage materials.

3. String sculpture together with wool or string. Several small structures can be joined together.

Note: If the sculpture is painted with a clear gloss enamel, the writing on the boxes will show through the paint.

OVER 3 YEARS

Soap sculpture

YOU WILL NEED:

2 cups soap flakes
½ cup hot water
Powder paint for colouring, if desired
Aluminium foil
Electric mixer

1. (Adult) add hot water to soap flakes and beat with mixer until stiff. A little paint may be added to flakes for colouring.

2. Dip hands into warm water before moulding with this mixture. If sculpture is made on aluminium foil it is easy to move. Soap sculpture dries to a porous texture and lasts for weeks. Collage materials may be stuck into it. On pine cones, it looks just like snow.

Sculpture, the creation of three dimensional structures, challenges a child's imagination. There are endless possibilities for constructing and modelling various materials into unusual and wonderful sculptures.

Simple Sculpture

Box dragon

YOU WILL NEED:

2 litre milk cartons (at least eight)
White and coloured paper
Pipe cleaners
Paper fasteners
P.V.A. glue
Scissors
Paint
Collage materials
Wool
Paintbrushes

1. (Adult) pull top of carton fully open. From this top section, cut away the two sides that are most creased. To remove these two flaps (which are opposite each other), cut around three creases of each. Repeat for each carton.

2. Cover outside of carton with white or coloured paper and tape into place. Paint cartons or glue on collage materials.

3. To make dragon's head, cut off all top folded section of a carton. Starting at one top corner, cut a deep V into a side of the carton to

about two-thirds of the way down, coming back up to the next top corner of the carton. Cut similarly on the opposite side of the carton. These are the dragon's jaws. Cover with paper and decorate with paint and collage materials. Eyes can be made out of egg carton cups or sea shells. Glue the eyes on top.

4. (Adult) to connect parts of the dragon, overlap top flaps of a carton onto the bottom of another milk carton. In the centre of this overlap, pierce two holes through both thicknesses of cartons with scissors. Push each end of a 10cm piece of pipe cleaner through each hole to inside of carton. Reach inside carton and twist together two ends of pipe cleaners. Repeat this process with other side of the two cartons to connect them. Alternatively, paper fasteners may be used instead of pipe cleaners. Threaded beads, bottle caps or macaroni may be added for a tail.

Boats

Boats can be made from a variety of household articles, including empty milk cartons, drinking straws, matchboxes and ice block sticks. For the battleship, the milk carton was covered with heavy duty aluminium foil. For the cruise liner, ring reinforcements were used for port holes. For the round boat, ice block sticks were cut in half and stuck with P.V.A. glue onto a plastic takeaway food container. The tug was covered with clear self-adhesive plastic. Masking tape can be used on milk carton seams to ensure vessels stay afloat. Other boats can be made by connecting pieces of polystyrene with heavy round-stemmed toothpicks. If these are not available, make holes in polystyrene with a darning needle or similar object then use ordinary toothpicks. Older children may also use kebab skewers. Colourful sails and flags are lively additions to the boats and they really float! Attach a string and pull.

73

Pea mobile

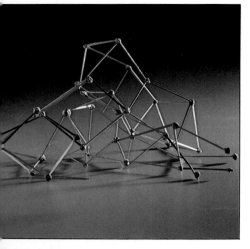

YOU WILL NEED:
Fresh pea pods
Coloured toothpicks, preferably
pointed at both ends (how to
dye, pages 4-5)
String

*Vegetables,
wire, boxes and
wood scraps are
all treasures for
young sculptors.*

1. Shell peas.

2. Stick toothpick into pea. Place pea on other end of toothpick and stick another toothpick into same pea. Continue this process to create a geometric structure. Take care that no more than four toothpicks are stuck into each pea because the pea will fall apart.

3. When finished, allow peas to dry out for several days. Do not touch them while they're drying.

4. Tie string to structure and hang string from ceiling.

ALL AGES

Pipe cleaners

YOU WILL NEED:
A variety of
pipe cleaners, all
colours, with
short or shaggy fur

1. Let your imagination loose and twist pipe cleaners into interesting animals and people.

2. Odds and ends can be used for eyes and clothes.

School's Out!

Holidays and rainy days are times for happily filling in the hours. Children can make gifts for the family or simply create decorative items to keep. Brightly painted rocks and pegs, papier mâché animals, skittles, paper wall hangings, high-flying kites and blueprint cards are fun to make. Pressed flowers and nature gardens make children aware of articles to collect on bush walks.

Paper bag kites

YOU WILL NEED:

Large paper bag
String
Paper ring reinforcements
Hole puncher
Paper collage materials
P.V.A. glue
Paint
Tissue paper and crepe
paper streamers

1. Punch hole on each of the four corners of paper bag (at least 3cm from edge of bag). Put paper ring reinforcement on each hole.

2. Cut two pieces of string to a length of about 80cm. Tie each end into a hole to form two loops.

3. Cut a piece of string about 80cm long. Put it through the two loops and tie it. It will act as a handle.

4. Bag can be painted as desired. Allow to dry.

5. Glue on paper collage materials and streamers. Allow to dry.

6. Open bag. Hold onto string and run so that wind catches in bag and makes the kite fly.

For variation, try a plastic bag.

Note: Younger children will need help with steps 1, 2 and 3.

COLLAGE KITE (left)

Cut a kite shape from an old painting or print. Glue on any lightweight collage material. Tie on a tail made from any stringing materials. Tie a string on other end of kite and holding on to it, run.

Papier mâché animals

YOU WILL NEED:

Balloons
Cardboard rolls, all sizes
Aluminium foil
Cardboard
Masking tape
Clean sand
Newspaper
Wallpaper paste
White paint or paper
Powder paint
Large and small paint brushes
Scissors
Clear gloss enamel

1. Make a general animal shape by taping together balloons (tied with a double knot), wads of foil, cardboard and cardboard rolls.

2. Tear newspaper into strips about 5cm × 15cm. Dip strips into wallpaper paste and stick onto animal shape. Cover shape with about four layers of newspaper. Allow to dry for several days.

3. If the animal shape doesn't sit up, cut a small hole in the bottom with scissors and puncture the balloon. Put about one cup of sand into the shape. Cover the hole with five or six layers of masking tape. The sand will make the animal shape sit upright.

4. Cover shape with white paint and allow to dry. The paint will prevent newsprint from showing through when the shape is glossed. Alternatively, the shape may be covered with white paper and paste, instead of paint.

5. Paint shape with main colour and allow to dry. Allowing it to dry between layers of paint prevents the colours from mixing. Paint on other colours and allow to dry. Using a small brush, paint on any details desired, such as eyes and nose. Allow to dry thoroughly.

6. (Adult) for a finished look, paint animal with clear gloss enamel.

OVER 3 YEARS

Bangles

YOU WILL NEED:

Cardboard
Wallpaper paste
Newspaper
White paint or paper
Powder paint
Coloured tissue paper
Liquid starch
Felt-tipped pens
Stapler
Scissors
Clear gloss enamel, if desired

Create a whole menagerie of papier mâché animals and fanciful fantasy creatures.

1. (Adult) cut a cardboard strip about 28cm long and as wide as a bangle, about 2cm to 4cm. Overlap the ends until the size fits over child's hand loosely, allow for thickness added by papier mâché. Staple ends together. Following directions on packet, mix up a small amount of wallpaper paste.

2. Tear newspaper into small strips about 2cm x 6cm. Dip a piece of newspaper into wallpaper paste and wrap around bangle. Repeat this process until the bangle has been covered all over with at least three layers of newspaper.

3. Cover the bangle with thin white paper or paint it with white paint when it is dry, otherwise the newsprint will show through, especially if the bangle is glossed. It may take several days for the papier mâché to dry. (Bangles may be placed in microwave on defrost cycle for 5-10 minutes to speed up drying).

4. Decorate bangles by painting or drawing on them or covering them with liquid starch and layers of coloured tissue paper.

5. (Adult) when dry, paint with clear gloss enamel.

Paper hangings

YOU WILL NEED:

Sheet of graph paper
Powder paint
String
Toothbrush
Paintbrush
Staples
P.V.A. glue
Comb or wire screen
Felt-tipped pens

1. To make fluted circles, concertina or fan-fold along heavy lines on rectangular piece of graph paper. Ours measured 72cm x 36cm.

2. Tie a piece of string at the centre of the folded paper and glue either side to make a circle.

3. Animal features such as ears may be cut out of other paper, folded, and stapled to the circle.

4. If spatter painting is to be used, cut stencils for shapes or features such as eyes and mouth. Place cut out stencils on circle and spatter paint by moving a toothbrush dipped in paint across a comb or wire screen.

5. Hand paint or draw details of animal features onto circle.

6. Attach string and hang on wall or tape an ice block stick to circle to make a fan.

Note: Younger children may need help with steps 1, 2 and 6.

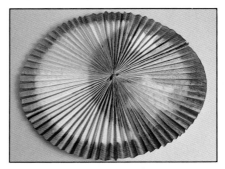

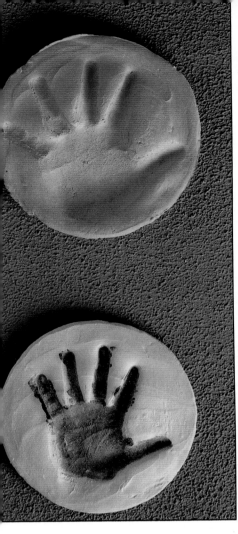

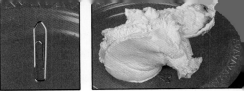

Plaster hands

YOU WILL NEED:

Paper or plastic plate
Casting plaster (available from a hardware shop and less expensive than plaster of Paris)
Water
Large paper clip
Powder paint
2 large icecream containers

1. Pour plaster powder into an icecream container (use about 500 grams per hand). Make only two to three hands at a time

2. Add paint powder if colour is desired. Add enough water so that consistency seems rough and cracked but smooths well when a spoon is run over the top. Make sure it is stirred thoroughly.

3. Bend paper clip as illustrated and place it near the top of plate. Scoop plaster into plate, press down and smooth over.

4. Plaster is ready when it holds the shape of a hole after a finger is pressed into it. Plaster is usually ready as soon as it is put in plate. Press hand into plaster and remove hand quickly.

5. Leave plaster overnight to harden. Remove from plate. Dig around paper clip a little so it can hang on a nail in the wall.

Nature garden

YOU WILL NEED:

Homemade or commercial play dough or casting plaster
Heavy paper plate
Flowers, gum nuts, twigs, rocks, weeds and so on
(these can be collected on a nature walk)

1. Spread play dough or casting plaster (available from a hardware shop) into bottom of paper plate.

2. Press leaves, flowers and other objects into play dough or plaster to make a nature garden.

For variation, make a miniature nature garden using a cup segment from an egg carton.

Play aquarium

YOU WILL NEED:

2 paper plates
Scissors
P.V.A. glue
Wool scraps
Felt-tipped pens or crayons
Stapler
Clear plastic wrap
Coloured cellophane
Sand, pebbles

1. (Adult) cut centre out of one paper plate, leaving narrow rim.

2. With the rim of the plate right side up, put a line of glue along the inside edge. Stretch clear plastic across the opening and glue it down to create a window effect. When dry, cut off excess plastic.

3. Cut out fish shapes from the discarded centre section of the plate.

4. Colour fish with felt-tipped pens or crayons. The underside of the rim can also be coloured.

5. Glue fish, wool, sand, cellophane onto the second plate.

6. Place first plate upside down on the other plate and staple all around the outside.

Pressed flowers

YOU WILL NEED:

Fresh flowers
Newspapers
Heavy books

Gather fresh flowers on a nature walk. Lay them out individually on a newspaper so they are not touching. Put several sheets of newspaper on top of them. Put books or any flat, heavy weight on top of the newspaper. Leave them about four weeks to dry out thoroughly. Thick flowers take longer.

Note: Pressed dried flower arrangements are delicate and should be handled with care.

WALL PICTURES

YOU WILL NEED:

Wooden curtain rings
Small pressed flowers
Heavy paper
P.V.A. glue
Toothpicks
Scissors
Pen
Scribble paper
Saucer

Discarded cicada wings and leaf skeletons make delicate and pretty patterns.

1. Place curtain ring on paper. Draw around outside of ring, keeping pen close to ring. Cut out circle about ½cm on the inside of the drawn circle.

2. Put a few drops of glue into saucer. Put paper circle on table with pressed flowers spread out near it. Choose one flower and place it upside down on scribble paper. Dip thicker end of toothpick into glue and apply lightly to back of the flower.

3. Carefully lift flower and place it glue side down on paper circle. Repeat this process to get desired arrangement of flowers.

4. Put curtain ring on table. Apply one circle of glue to back of ring (a squeeze bottle is easiest). Lift up ring and place it glue side down on top of flower arrangement (with the screw eye at the top of the arrangement). The ring becomes a frame for the arrangement. The screw eye can hang on a wall hook.

Box car

YOU WILL NEED:

Large cardboard box with top flaps cut off
Powder paint
Paintbrushes
6 paper plates
Heavy string or cord
Aluminium foil
Paper fasteners, about 2cm in length
Small polystyrene packing tray
Stapler
Tape
Scissors
Felt-tipped pen

1. (Adult) cut a hole in bottom of box large enough to slip over a child's hips.

2. Mix powder paint with water. With hole on top, paint box. Allow to dry.

3. (Adult) pierce four holes in box with scissors at point where wheels are to be attached. Pierce holes in centre of four paper plates. Attach plates to sides of box with paper fasteners. Cover pointed ends of fasteners inside box with tape.

4. Use two metal pie plates or two smaller paper plates covered with foil as headlights. (Adult) pierce hole through centre of plates and front of box with scissors. Attach plates to box with paper fasteners or tape. Cover pointed ends of fasteners inside box with tape.

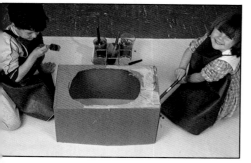

Make a train by adding more boxes as carriages. Turn boxes upside-down on the ground, behind one another, and children can climb aboard the train for a ride.

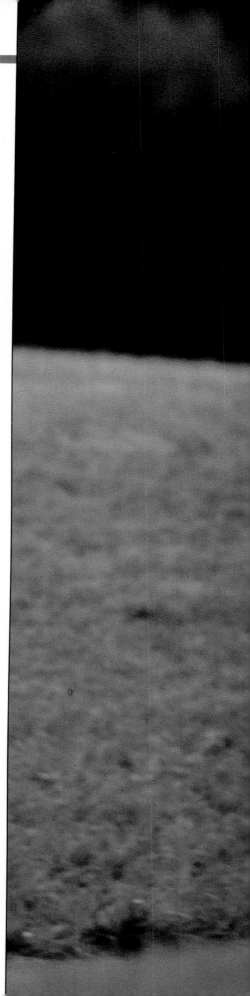

5. Write your name on packing tray with felt-tipped pen. Attach to back of box with staples or tape.

6. (Adult) in centre of each side on top of box, pierce a hole with scissors. Thread string or cord through one hole. Tie a double knot so it cannot slip through hole.

7. Step into box and pull it up to the waist. (Adult) pull string or cord around back of child's neck and through second hole. Tie a double knot to secure string or cord. The car is ready for a ride.

Tie dyeing

YOU WILL NEED:
Cotton fabric (sheet, T-shirt, pillowcase for example)
Rubber bands (thick and thin)
Multi-purpose dye
Saucepan with water
Stove
Salt

Every tie-dyed design is different — use it to brighten up plain coloured serviettes, pillowcases or tea towels.

Note: Check dye packet to see what other fabrics, in addition to cotton, are suitable to dye.

1. Bunch a piece of fabric in one hand and twist rubber band tightly around it. Repeat this process all over the fabric. (The fabric under the rubber bands will not be affected by the dye and will remain the original colour.)

2. Submerge fabric in water so that it is completely wet.

3. (Adult) following directions on packet, mix up dye. Place garment into dye and put on stove for time specified on packet. Salt in the dye solution and the simmering process will help the garment to become colour fast.

4. Remove garment from dye, rinse under running tap until water is clear. Take off rubber bands.

5. If another colour is desired, repeat step 1. When choosing a second colour, bear in mind the final colour that will result from adding the two colours together.

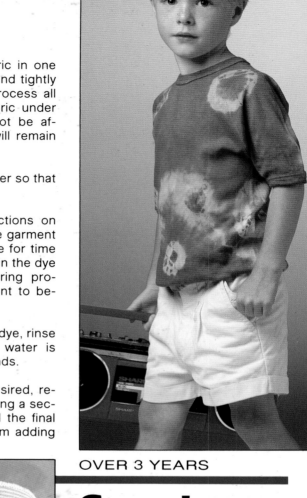

Serviette rings

YOU WILL NEED:
Cardboard tube
Powder paint
Tissue paper
Knife
Clear gloss enamel
Liquid starch

1. (Adult) cut tube into sections, about 5cm in length.

2. Paint with powder paint. Allow to dry, apply another coat.

3. Paint designs on the cut sections or apply tissue paper collage with liquid starch.

4. When dry, (adult) coat with clear gloss enamel.

Box puzzle

YOU WILL NEED:
Sheet of paper
Empty matchboxes
Felt-tipped pens
Scissors
P.V.A. glue
Ruler
Child's drawing or painting

1. Select a favourite drawing or painting, preferably one that is simple but solidly coloured.

2. (Adult) using the ruler, mark off the sizes of the matchboxes on the back of the drawing — most matchboxes are 5.3cm × 3.8cm.

Across the top of the paper place a mark every 5.3cm. Down the side of the paper place a mark every 3.8cm. Draw vertical and horizontal lines on the paper to make boxes.

3. Following the lines, cut out the rectangles. Glue each square drawing to the top of each matchbox. Arrange the boxes to make the original drawing.

Blue print pictures

YOU WILL NEED:

Large glass or plastic jar with screw top
Household ammonia (NB: poisonous)
Ammonia Diazo paper, cut to fit into jar without touching ammonia in bottom of jar
Large, thin hardback book
Sheet of glass with taped edges, a little larger than Diazo paper
Flat leaves, ferns, flowers
Steel wool (not soap pads)
Sunlight (not early morning or late afternoon)

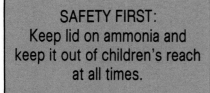

SAFETY FIRST:
Keep lid on ammonia and keep it out of children's reach at all times.

These pictures make attractive greeting cards. Get Diazo paper scraps from your friendly architect or from a plan printing materials shop. Paper comes with either blue or black images; blue is a little more dramatic. Store paper in sealed envelope in a dark place to keep it light sensitive.

1. (Adult) pour 1cm of ammonia into jar. Pull steel wool apart so that it will cover bottom of jar and touch sides of jar but still be at least 3cm thick. Place steel wool into jar, taking care not to breathe in ammonia. The steel wool will keep paper dry but still allow ammonia fumes to get to paper. Place ammonia out of reach.

2. In a room with no direct sunlight and no electric light on, place book on top of table. Place paper on top of book with yellow side up. Place flat objects on top of paper. Place glass on top of flat objects.

3. Firmly grasp both sides (all layers). Walk into direct sunlight and wait 30 seconds. Return to darkened room holding all layers firm.

4. (Adult) remove paper and roll up with exposed side out. Place paper in jar and quickly replace lid. The ammonia fumes develop the blue print pictures in less than one minute. After a minute, remove paper and replace lid.

For a crisp, sharp image it is essential objects are held firmly. If objects move, the image becomes blurred and fuzzy.

This project is easier when done with small groups of children.

Make your own stationery or set of place mats by covering prints with self-adhesive plastic.

Note pad

YOU WILL NEED:

Note pad
Pencil with groove cut
into top end
String or wool
Paper fasteners (thumb tacks
for wood)
Paint or tissue paper and liquid
starch, or fabric scraps cut in
squares and other shapes
Rectangular piece of heavy
cardboard or wood (larger than
note pad)
Small dried flowers (optional)
Wall hanging hooks
P.V.A. glue
Rick rack tape

1. Decorate the cardboard or wood with tissue paper and starch, paint, or glue fabric scraps on and finish the edges with rick rack. Dry.

2. Glue note pad to cardboard or wood. (Adult) pierce hole in cardboard and stick paper fastener through. A thumb tack is better for wood. Wrap one end of string around pin or tack. (Adult) cut groove into top end of pencil and tie other end of string around pencil groove so that it won't slip off.

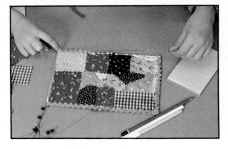

3. (Adult) put wall hanging hooks on back of wood or glue wall hanger on back of cardboard.

89

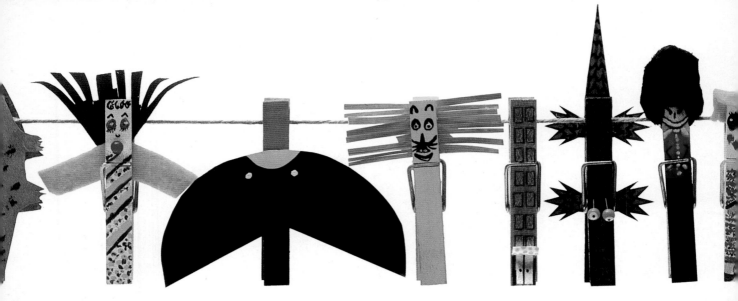

Pegs

YOU WILL NEED:

Wooden spring
clothes pegs
Paint
Paintbrushes
Felt-tipped pens
Crepe paper
Paper
Fabric scraps
Cotton wool
P.V.A. glue

Paint peg any colour. Draw on features. Add pieces of cotton wool, fabric, crepe paper or wool to make a creature or person. There is no end of possibilities when making peg creatures: crocodiles, lions, Santa Claus, buildings, birds, boys and girls and clowns and many, many more. What can you think of?

Rock painting

YOU WILL NEED:

Smooth rocks
Powder paint
Paintbrushes
Pipe cleaners
P.V.A. glue
Clear gloss enamel or
spray varnish

1. Paint any abstract or animal design onto rock (e.g cat, mouse, fish, owl, flower, human face or beetle). Allow to dry thoroughly.

2. If desired, glue on pipe cleaners for tails, feelers or legs.

3. (Adult) paint rock with clear gloss enamel or spray with varnish.

Earth clay (page 69) can be painted in same way after it has dried out.

Skittles

YOU WILL NEED:

Several empty plastic cordial
or similar bottles
Clean sand
Newspaper
Wallpaper paste
(or cornflour and water paste)
Wool and other
collage materials
Paint
P.V.A glue
Funnel
Clear gloss enamel

1. Crumple a double sheet of newspaper into a roughly round shape for the head, pulling out a longish piece for the neck.

2. Using the funnel, fill each plastic bottle about one-third full of sand. The sand helps prevent bottles from falling over too easily.

3. Paste newspaper strips all over the head and down onto the neck, which will end up sitting in the neck of the bottle.

4. Paint eyes, nose and mouth on head, stick on wool for hair.

5. Paint the bottle base with colourful designs. Decorate with collage materials. (Adult) paint with clear gloss enamel.

6. Stand the skittles up and try to knock them over with a ball. Add up your score.

For variation, use plastic cream containers to make skittles. Half-fill one cream container with sand. Replace lid and join two containers at the neck with tape or glue. To make a skittle head, tape or glue polystyrene ball to flat end of container on top. Tear newspaper into biggish pieces. Place pieces into wallpaper paste and cover them completely with paste. Take pieces out and place them around containers and ball. Cover containers completely with a couple of layers of newspaper pieces. Allow to dry for a few days. When dry, paint skittles white or a pale colour — the head can be left white or painted. Paint eyes, nose and mouth on head or stick on buttons or plastic eyes and add wool for hair. Paint containers and decorate them with collage materials. If desired, (adult) paint skittles with clear gloss enamel to preserve them.

Vegetable sculpture

YOU WILL NEED:

Coloured toothpicks (how to dye, pages 4-5)
Apples, oranges and various fruits
Carrots, potatoes and various vegetables
Sultanas
Marshmallows
Soft sweets
Pipe cleaners

Using the toothpicks, stick a selection of fruits and vegetables together to form a sculpture or a creature. Choose foods that will be easy to stick toothpicks into; avoid hard foods. Vegetables could be cooked slightly so that they are more easily pierced by sharp objects such as toothpicks.

Note: Children may be encouraged to eat healthy foods if they are presented in a fun way. The salad clown (right) is made of mashed potatoes, lettuce, hard-boiled eggs, alfalfa, carrots, capsicum, olives, tomato, chives, cucumber and radish. Make your own version.

Fun with Food

Treats to eat

RICE BUBBLE CREATURES
YOU WILL NEED:

Rice Bubbles
50g butter or margarine
250g packet of marshmallows
Electric frypan
Spoon
Currants, glace cherries,
licorice, peppermints, candied
citrus pieces
Pipe cleaners
Aluminium foil

1. (Adult) with frypan on medium low, melt butter/margarine. Add marshmallows and continue stirring until marshmallows are melted, or microwave together on high for 2 minutes.

2. (Adult) while stirring, add enough Rice Bubbles to make a stiff consistency (approximately 2-3 cups). Turn frypan off.

3. Tear off large pieces of foil (about 30cm) for each child. Lightly grease foil.

4. (Adult) scoop a large spoonful of mixture onto each piece of foil.

5. Put a little butter on inside of hands. While mixture is just warm (not hot), mould into desired shape. Decorate as desired.

DRIED FRUIT FIGURES

Dried apricots, apples, prunes, figs, dates, peaches, sultanas and orange peel can be strung together on thread to form puppet characters, caterpillars, snakes and other curious creatures. Here, we used dried apricots for the legless caterpillar, with pipe cleaners for antennae, dried figs and prunes for Mr Spider (with slivered almonds for fangs, glace cherry eyes). The prune snake was strung together on pipe cleaners. Dried fruit figures can be eaten and make delightful Christmas gifts from children.

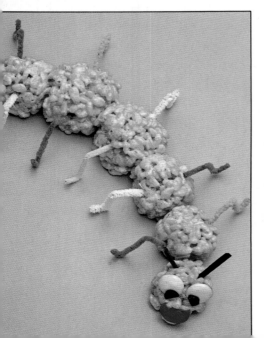

SWEET INSECTS

YOU WILL NEED:

Kitchen clear plastic wrap
Coloured pipe cleaners
Sweets, such as freckles,
licorice-all-sorts,
Smarties, candy bananas

1. Place sweets on strips of plastic wrap and wind the wrap around them to form shapes.

2. Twist pipe cleaners at appropriate intervals to form head, bodies and legs.
These quaint creatures are great for birthday party table decoration or for hanging with other baubles on the Christmas tree.

Icing ideas

ROYAL ICING

YOU WILL NEED:
1¼ cups pure icing sugar
1 egg white
½ teaspoon lemon juice

Method: (adult) have egg white at room temperature. Sift icing sugar and measure it. Beat egg white lightly in a small bowl, using a wooden spoon. Add sifted icing sugar a tablespoon at a time, beating well after each addition. When icing reaches desired consistency, add lemon juice which is necessary for quick drying. Beat well. The amount of icing sugar required depends on size of egg white and consistency of icing required. Excess icing can be stored in an airtight container in the refrigerator for about a week and used again.

Things to make: face (left), or stick biscuits, marshmallows, sweets and pipe cleaners together with icing to make animals, automobiles (below) or other unusual creations.

MARZIPAN FRUITS

YOU WILL NEED:

Marzipan
Food colouring
Whole cloves

1. Break marzipan into about five balls. Add a little food colouring to each ball and work the colouring in with your hands.

2. Using the coloured marzipan, make miniature oranges, bananas, plums, watermelons, and other fruits. Add leaves and whole cloves for stems. Store marzipan fruits covered with plastic wrap.

Chocolates

YOU WILL NEED:

200g dark chocolate
1 teaspoon vegetable oil
50g chopped nuts
50g sultanas
50g chopped glace cherries

Method: (adult) melt the chocolate over a double boiler, or microwave on high for 1 minute. Place chocolate in another container. Child may then add the oil and stir until smooth. Combine the chocolate, fruit and nuts. Spoon into paper patty cups and refrigerate until set.

Paper bag piñata

Real piñatas, made from pottery and originating in Mexico, are centrepieces at celebrations. They are filled with sweets, tiny presents, flowers and other treasures. When they are hit with a stick, piñatas explode into fragments and shower their contents into the uplifted hands of party guests. For children, piñatas are made to be broken more easily, as on this page, with the simple paper bag example. Slightly more sturdy piñatas, using papier mâché techniques, are on following pages. Adult help may be required for very young children.

YOU WILL NEED:

Paper bags
Newspaper
Inexpensive wallpaper paste or liquid starch
String, about 1 metre in length
Tissue paper
Crepe paper
Paint (powder paint covers newsprint well)
Sweets
Scissors
Stick, about 1 metre in length and 3cm thick
Blindfold

1. Scrunch up newspaper and stuff paper bag with it to make it firm. Tie end of paper bag with string.

2. Cover bag with paint and/or tissue paper applied with liquid starch or paste. If desired, take crepe paper and fold several times to form a 5cm strip. On one fold make repeated 3cm cuts close together. Run fingers across loops to separate them a little. With loops pointing up, glue uncut side around bag. Allow to dry.

3. Untie end of bag and remove newspaper. Fill bag with sweets and retie string.

4. (Adult) tie bag to ceiling with string, keeping bag well down from ceiling so as not to cause any damage with stick. Child wearing a blindfold stands near piñata and swings at it with stick, trying to break it open. After four or five attempts, the blindfold and stick should be given to another child to try to break piñata. When piñata breaks open, sweets will fall out for children to collect.
All spectators should stand well clear of the child with the stick!
At a party it is a good idea to have one piñata for every four children so that each child gets a turn at trying to break it.

The paper bag piñata is very simple to make. Other good party ideas: face painting, dressing up and treasure hunts.

Party Time

For a children's party, entertain young guests with games centred around articles they've made themselves. Piñatas may be made by the young host or hostess; the guests at a masked party will love making and wearing their own homemade fantasy masks. A variety of musical instruments are also fun to make and play with.

Papier mâché balloon

YOU WILL NEED:

Inexpensive wallpaper paste
Newspaper
Balloon
Paint (powder paint covers
newsprint well)

1. Blow up balloon and tie a double knot in the end.

2. Following instructions on the packet, mix up wallpaper paste.

3. Tear newspaper into strips. Place a few strips into wallpaper paste and cover them completely with paste. Take one strip from paste and wrap it around balloon. Repeat process until balloon has about three layers of paper around it. Allow to dry thoroughly (it takes one or two days, depending on layers of newspaper).

4. Paint colourful design on balloon. Allow to dry thoroughly.

5. Balloon can be coated with lacquer or clear gloss enamel.

PAPIER MÂCHÉ FISH PIÑATA

YOU WILL NEED:

Balloon
Coloured newsprint or
newspaper
Collage materials
Strips of crepe
and cellophane paper
Powder paint
Wallpaper paste
Scissors

1. Blow up balloon and tie a double knot in the end.

2. Following instructions on packet, mix up wallpaper paste.

3. Tear paper into biggish pieces. Cover balloon with about four layers of coloured newsprint or ordinary newspaper, following instructions, step 3, papier mâché balloon, left.

4. Paint piñata with bright colours, to make fish, bird, animal or abstract creation. Stick on streamers for decoration.

5. When dry, (adult) cut a small lid in the top, prick balloon and pull it out. Fill hollow with sweets.

The papier mâché koala piñata was made by preschool children. Fish and birds are also popular shapes. We've even seen a wombat!

Musical instruments

The photograph at left shows children with (from back) rhythm sticks, balloon shaker, tamborine, string instrument (instructions over page), bell and paper shakers.

TAMBORINE

YOU WILL NEED:

2 plastic plates or 3 uncoated paper plates
P.V.A. glue
Hole puncher
Wool
Metal bottle caps with a hole punched in them (sea shells or similar noisy items may also be used)
Crepe paper or coloured tissue paper streamers
Paint
Paintbrushes
Tape or stapler

1. Glue plates together for added strength. Paint paper plates.

2. (Adult) punch holes around rim of plate, about 5cm apart.

3. Thread wool through holes around plate, adding two bottle caps at a time in five or six places.

4. (Adult) tie ends of the wool together in a knot.

5. Tape or staple crepe paper or tissue streamers around wool.

COCONUT CLAPPERS

After an adult has cut a coconut shell in half and removed the coconut flesh, children can paint the shell halves. Adult should then paint them with clear gloss enamel. A child holds a coconut half in each hand and hits them together to make a clapping sound.

BOTTLE SHAKERS

Put ½ cup of dried beans, corn or other similiar items into empty plastic bottles. Replace lid. Decorate with collage materials and P.V.A. glue or tissue paper applied with liquid starch.

BELL SHAKER

YOU WILL NEED:

Cardboard roll, about 15cm in length
Hole puncher
Powder paint or tissue paper and liquid starch
Paintbrushes
Metal jingle bells
Clear gloss enamel

1. (Adult) punch holes about 1cm apart around one end of roll.

2. Decorate roll with paint or tissue paper applied with liquid starch. (Adult) cover powder paint with coat of clear gloss enamel so paint will not rub off.

3. Thread wool through holes in roll adding bells in three or four places.

4. (Adult) tie ends of wool in a knot.

For variation, glue or staple foil or paper streamers to one end of roll to make a paper shaker.

RHYTHM STICKS

These are easily made by painting long pieces of dowling, about 30cm long and 1cm to 2cm thick. When dry, adult can coat sticks with clear gloss enamel. Hit sticks together in time to music.

BALLOON SHAKER

Make a papier mâché balloon (see page 100). When thoroughly dry, an adult can cut a small hole and puncture balloon. Put in ½ cup of dried beans, corn, sand or anything to make a shaking sound. Put at least four layers of masking tape over hole. Paint shaker with white paint (to prevent newsprint showing through) and allow to dry. Cover with coloured paint and dry. (Adult) coat with clear gloss enamel to stop paint rubbing off.

PIE PLATE SHAKERS

YOU WILL NEED:

Coloured wool on darning needle with knot tied in end
Metal pie plates (put one plate inside another for strength if they are thin)
Dried beans or other dried food
P.V.A. glue
Cut paper shapes or any collage materials

1. Place one plate face down on top of other. Loop stitch around outside with wool about 1cm apart. Before completely sewing up plates, put dried food inside to make shaking noise. Sew up the remaining space.

2. Glue on cut paper shapes (see page 121) and other decorations.

Note: Younger children may need help with sewing.

Musical instruments

STRING INSTRUMENT
(pictured previous page)

YOU WILL NEED:

Heavy small box without lid
(shoe box is a good size)
Rubber bands of different
thicknesses and widths
Collage materials
Paint
Paintbrushes

1. Decorate box as desired.

2. Put rubber bands around box.

3. Strum rubber bands.

SILVER GUITAR

*This is a more sophisticated
version of the string instrument
and is better suited to children
over the age of 5.*

YOU WILL NEED:

Strong cardboard box, similar
size to a shoe box
Cardboard tube roll, about
35cm in length
Aluminium foil
Long rubber bands
Scissors
2 pencils
Tape

1. (Adult) cut a hole in lid of box
leaving about a 5cm strip at sides
and 3cm at top and bottom.

2. (Adult) cut a hole in one end of
box large enough to fit cardboard
roll through.

3. Cover roll with foil. Place it
through hole in box and tape it in
place.

4. Tape lid to box. Cover box with
foil. Cut away foil from hole in lid.

5. String rubber bands from one
end of box to the other.

6. Place pencils covered in foil
under all the bands at each end to
give a better sound.

Decorate guitar with paint mixed
with dishwashing liquid or glue on
magazine cutouts or tissue paper.

DRUM

YOU WILL NEED:

Empty tin can with lid cut off
Brown wrapping paper
White paper
Paper paste
Masking tape
Foil, tissue paper or children's
old drawings
Collage materials
Paint
Paintbrushes
Saucepan lid, larger than tin
Scissors

1. Place saucepan lid on wrapping
paper and trace around it. Trace
about eight more circles and cut
them out.

2. Place circle of paper over open
end of can. Fold paper around
sides of can and tape into place.

3. Brush paper paste onto paper
top and place another circle of
paper on top and tape into place
around sides of can. Repeat until
top is strong (usually eight or nine
layers). Allow to dry.

4. Cover can with white paper and
secure with tape. Decorate with
collage materials, foil or paint.

To make a drumstick: Cover top of
tablespoon with cotton wool.
Cover cotton wool with piece of
fabric, about 10cm square, and secure with rubber bands.

XYLOPHONE

A delightful xylophone can be made using glass bottles filled with coloured water. We used six fruit juice bottles but milk bottles are just as good. Fill each bottle with water to varying levels and add a few drops of food colouring. Gently strike each bottle with a pencil or spoon to get different notes.

Masks

Children enjoy dressing up and pretending they are someone else — masks help them to take on a new personality. Masks are easily made by using paper plates, paper bags and cardboard shapes which can then be tied around the head. Children also have a lot of fun wearing a body mask made out of a plastic open-mesh upright laundry basket. Paper and sticks may be tied to it and the basket put over the child's head. It's easy to see through the gaps in the mesh while remaining disguised. Here we show you a few ideas for different masks for make-believe.

CIRCLE MASKS
YOU WILL NEED:

Cardboard or paper plate
Crepe paper
Large plate or saucepan lid
Paint
Paintbrushes
Scissors
P.V.A. glue
Wool or elastic
Felt-tipped pens

1. Draw a circle on cardboard using large plate or saucepan lid. (Adult) cut out circle. Make incision from edge to centre and overlap pieces to form a slight peak in centre of cardboard. Glue overlapping pieces together. Paint cardboard any colour desired to make an animal or human face. Allow to dry.

2. (Adult) cut strips of crepe paper or wool for hair. Glue strips to front and back of edge of cardboard.

3. Paint or draw a face on outside of cardboard circle.

4. (Adult) cut holes for eyes and mouth and at side of mask to thread wool or elastic through. Thread wool or elastic, tie around back of child's head.

Happy Easter Ideas

Bunnies and bonnets and, above all, beautifully coloured and decorated eggs symbolise the festive side of Easter, all over the world. Here are several bright ideas for making your own Easter eggs, including batik and onion skin dyed examples. Or try our pretty baskets and easy-to-make bonnets.

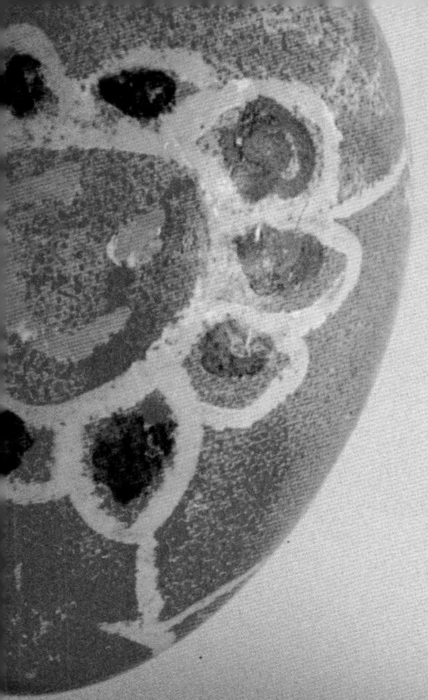

Crayon-resist dyeing

YOU WILL NEED:

Hard-boiled eggs
Crayons
Easter egg dye or multi-
purpose fabric dye or crepe
paper dye (page 111)
Cup
Spoons
Aluminium foil

1. Using crayons, draw designs onto eggs. Heavier lines will show up more after dyeing.

2. Following directions on packet, mix up ⅔ of a cup of strong dye or use crepe paper dye as used on batik eggs. If dye is warm, wait for it to cool (warm dye will melt the crayon wax).

3. Using spoon, put egg into dye. It should be completely covered. Lift it out to check colour. Leave it until desired colour is reached (usually a few minutes). Lift egg out with spoon and place on a wrinkled piece of aluminium foil to dry.

Batik egg

YOU WILL NEED:

Fresh raw eggs, or
whole hard-boiled eggs
Crepe paper
Hot water
1 tablespoon of white vinegar
Candle
Leaves
Stocking
Matches

We "blew" raw eggs by making a small hole with a pin in both ends of the egg and blowing out the contents (it takes a bit of puff!). This way the yolks and whites can be used in cooking. However, the blown egg is quite fragile and if you prefer, whole eggs can be used. They should keep indefinitely, as the contents of eggs will dry up odourlessly, unless shell cracks.

Eggheads

YOU WILL NEED:

Hard-boiled eggs
Alfalfa or quick-growing seed
Cotton wool
Coloured felt-tipped pen or
poster paint

1. Paint faces on the shells carefully as the eggs are very fragile.

2. (Adult) cut top off egg neatly. Remove egg from shell.

3. Fill empty shell with cotton wool.

4. Sprinkle alfalfa on the top of the cotton wool and moisten well.

5. Cover with a small wad of moistened cotton wool and place eggs in a cup near a window. The seeds should sprout in a day or so and continue to grow for three or four days. Moisten cotton wool daily and remove top layer when sprouts have grown, to allow the "hair" to stand up straight.

1. To make the dye, cut strips of crepe paper about 2cm wide and place in a bowl. (Adult) cover with hot water to release the dye.

2. Remove paper and add one tablespoon of white vinegar to set the dye. Allow to cool.

3. (Adult) if you wish to leave any sections of the egg shell surface its natural colour, drip candle wax onto that area.

4. The eggs are decorated with several applications of wax and dye. Start with the lightest colour and work to the darkest. Dip the egg in the lightest dye (yellow, perhaps) until it is the desired colour. Dry with a tissue.

5. (Adult) drip wax onto the sections you want to keep yellow. Dip egg in the darker dye and dry with a tissue. It may take a few minutes to reach the desired colour.

6. (Adult) to remove wax, place egg on a tray in a moderate oven. When wax has melted (about two minutes), wipe dry with a tissue.

For variation, make leaf-printed eggs. Take a small piece of fern or ivy and hold it onto the egg. Secure the plant in place by wrapping a piece of stocking very firmly around the egg. Tie top of stocking with elastic band and dip egg in dye. Remove excess dye with a tissue and, when dry, peel off stocking and leaves to reveal pattern.

SAFETY FIRST
Because hot water and hot wax are involved, adult supervision is necessary.

Easter baskets

ALUMINIUM FOIL
YOU WILL NEED:

Aluminium foil
Any container to use as basket
Thick powder paint with a small amount of dishwashing liquid added, about 1 teaspoon per ½ cup paint. (This helps paint to stick to foil)
Small paintbrushes

1. Tear a piece of foil off roll. Place on table. Put container in middle and bring foil up around sides, over top and partially down inside of container. Trim excess if necessary. Press foil close to container.

2. Paint designs onto foil with paintbrushes. Allow to dry.

Note: If paint doesn't stick, add more dishwashing liquid. This will help it to stick to any slippery surface including plastic or tin.

GROWING GRASS
Start preparing basket three weeks before the Easter holiday.

YOU WILL NEED:

Plastic container (empty margarine or icecream container)
Lawn seed
Potting soil
Water
Tissue paper scraps
Liquid starch in a bowl
Paintbrush

1. Put 3cm or more of potting soil into plastic container. Sprinkle lawn seed thickly on top of soil so that seeds almost touch. Cover seeds with a thin layer of soil.

2. Water seeds lightly as described on packet and continue to keep surface moist every day. Place grass basket in a light spot. The outside of the basket may be decorated a few days before Easter by painting it with liquid starch and covering it with tissue paper scraps in various shapes. Tissue can be applied in several layers, using the starch as a glue.

MAKING THE HANDLES
Handles can be made of cord, heavy wool, ribbon or braided crepe paper. Staple them to each side of Easter basket. Large baskets should have two handles to ensure good balance.

Onion skin egg dyeing

YOU WILL NEED:

Eggs
Brown or purple onion skins
20 cm squares of old cloth
Small leaves or rice
Rubber bands
Pot for boiling eggs

1. Place cloth on table. Put about six layers of onion skins on top of cloth. Place leaves or bits of rice on top of onion skins.

2. Place egg on top of skins, leaves and rice and place more onion skins on top. Wrap cloth around it firmly. Wrap a number of rubber bands around the cloth to keep it in place and to press the onion skins firmly against the egg.

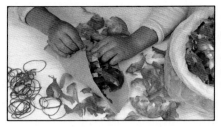

3. (Adult) put the wrapped egg in a pot of water and keep at boiling point for about 30 minutes.

4. Remove the egg from the water, leave to cool. Remove cloth and materials. When the egg is dry it can be rubbed with a little cooking oil to give it a shiny appearance.

Bonnets

YOU WILL NEED:
Children's old paintings
Crepe paper
Scissors
Coloured wool
Tissue paper or cellophane
Aluminium foil
Any collage materials
Silk or plastic flowers
Staples
P.V.A. glue

1. Select a pattern for the hat. (Adult) trace pattern onto an old painting. Cut hat out.

2. Glue collage materials and flowers onto hat. Allow to dry.

3. (Adult) attach crepe paper or wool to each side of hat and tie under chin.
For variation, cover hat shapes with foil before decorating.

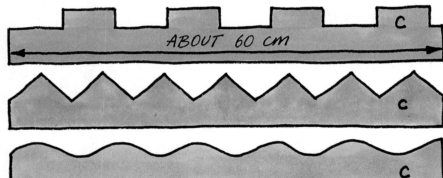

ABOUT 60 CM

C

C

C

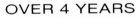

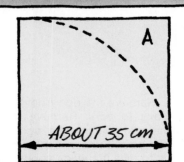

A

ABOUT 35 CM

B

CUT

ABOUT 40 CM

Note: It is easier to decorate bonnets before they are stapled together.

Hat A: Roll paper into a cone and staple at bottom. Staple a ribbon or crepe paper streamer on each side to act as a tie.

Hat B: Make a cut from edge of circle to centre. Overlap two pieces by about 8cm to form a slight peak, similar to a Chinese style hat. Staple together. Staple ribbons to inside of hat. To make a bonnet, overlap pieces about 20cm to 25cm. Staple together. Staple ribbons on right and left outside edges to act as a tie under chin.

Hat C: Fit cutout shape around child's head to get correct size. Staple ends together.

Bunnies

Create adorable Easter bunnies from cardboard or polystyrene balls. Add cuddly cotton wool, pipe cleaners, buttons or stick-on eyes. Draw a bunny onto a piece of cardboard and make a stand for it by taping one end of a rectangular piece of cardboard to the back of

Egg tree

Hard-boiled eggs
Pipe cleaners
Felt-tipped pens
Tree branch, about 1 metre
in length
Bucket of sand
Pastel powder paint
Knife
Spoon

1. Place branch into bucket of sand. Paint with pastel paint.

2. (Adult) cut tops off eggs. Scoop out egg very gently.

3. Using paint or pens, colour designs on outside of egg shells. Tissue paper may also be stuck onto egg shells for decoration.

4. (Adult) very gently, stick a pin through bottom of egg to make a small hole. Carefully push a pipe cleaner through hole. Bend end over to keep it inside egg.

5. Curve end of pipe cleaner to form a hook. Hang the eggs all over the painted branch.
Keep tree throughout the year for holiday celebrations. Decorate your tree with whatever children feel symbolises a special occasion.

the drawing and folding it at a right angle. Polystyrene balls make wonderfully rotund bunnies; cut a slice from the bottom of a ball to make it sit flat or tape it to cardboard. Stick pipe cleaners into the ball after making a small hole with a toothpick. Cardboard tubes make unusual bunnies; draw a face on the tube or glue on a cardboard face, cutout ears and other features.

Advent boxes

YOU WILL NEED:

24 small boxes of varying sizes
(matchboxes are good)
Christmas paper scraps and
children's paintings
Red and green crinkly gift
wrapping ribbon
Tape
Sweets, nuts, sultanas or
small toys
24 labels
Pen
Scissors

Advent is the season before Christmas. Advent boxes are small boxes which are filled with sweets and little suprises, wrapped up, and numbered from one to 24. As the countdown to Christmas begins on December 1, a present is opened each day until Christmas Eve.

1. Fill each box with sweets, nuts or small toys.

2. Wrap each box individually with wrapping paper and secure box with tape.

3. Tie each box with ribbon and a bow. Curl loose ends of ribbon by holding ribbon firmly between thumb and back of scissors and pulling ribbon through with your free hand.

4. Write a number from one to 24 on each label. Label each box.

5. Cut 24 long pieces of ribbon. Tie one end onto each box. Adjust the boxes so they hang at different lengths. Take all the ribbons at the top in one hand and divide them in half. Tie halves together with a double knot and a large bow. Curl all the ends of the loose ribbon.

6. Hang up and open each box on the appropriately numbered day before Christmas.

Christmas Trimmings

Christmas is an exciting and joyous time for children and they adore being involved in the preparations. Splendidly decorative treasures can be made for the Christmas tree using the simplest of materials . . . aluminium foil pie plates, glitter, dried pine cones, paper snowflakes, cutout Christmas cards, ornaments made from polystyrene trays. Some of these creations can be kept for years, becoming objects of pride. Here are some ideas for festive adornment, including a spectacular wall hanging of Advent boxes, at left, to be hung up 24 days before Christmas.

Tree decorations

DRY FOOD ORNAMENTS

YOU WILL NEED:

Cardboard
Hole puncher
Ribbon
P.V.A. glue
Coloured and uncoloured
pasta shapes
Gold or silver spray paint,
if desired

1. (Adult) draw Christmas shapes onto cardboard.

2. Cut out shapes. Glue several identical shapes together for added strength. Punch or make hole in one end of ornament.

3. Glue pasta onto one side. If desired, pasta can be glued onto other side. Other appropriate collage materials may be used. Allow glue to dry.

4. (Adult) if desired, spray with gold or silver paint and dry. Supervision and well-ventilated area is essential for safety reasons.

5. Thread ribbon through hole and hang on tree.

METAL PIE PLATES

YOU WILL NEED:

Small aluminium foil pie plates with hole punched (with a pencil or end of a paint brush) near the edge for hanging
P.V.A. glue
Glitter
String or ribbon

1. Apply glue to pie plates (either side for different effects). Apply glitter to glued areas. Shake off excess glitter. Allow to dry.

2. Thread ribbon through hole and tie ornament onto tree.

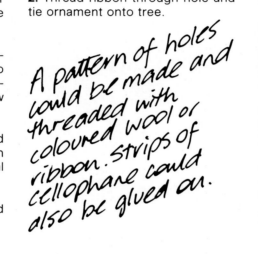

A pattern of holes could be made and threaded with coloured wool or ribbon. Strips of cellophane could also be glued on.

EGG CUP BELLS

YOU WILL NEED:

Egg carton cut into cups
Glitter
Glue (clear craft glue runs less)
Aluminium foil
Coloured pipe cleaners
Branch of tree upright in a
bucket of sand

1. Cut a circle from foil about 15cm in diameter. Place egg cup in centre of circle and wrap foil around it loosely so that irregularities in its shape are not too noticeable. Press gently.

2. Apply glue to foil and sprinkle with glitter. Other collage materials may be glued on but paint cannot be successfully applied to foil that is very wrinkled or lumpy.

3. (Adult) pierce hole in top of bell with scissors or other sharply pointed instrument.

4. Place a pipe cleaner through the hole in each bell and bend the end inside so bell will not slip off. A jingle bell can be attached to pipe cleaner inside. Bend a hook shape into other end and hang the bell on branch or Christmas tree.

More decorations

WRAPPING PRESENTS

Paintings and prints make appealing wrapping paper. Interesting cut paper decoration may be added by folding paper as in the snowflakes. They may be cut as in the snowflakes, or deep cuts may be made on the outside raw edge only. They stick onto packages easily with double-sided tape. For variation, use aluminium foil to wrap presents and cover it with snowflakes, star shapes (see opposite page) or other decorative materials.

HAIRPIN ORNAMENTS

YOU WILL NEED:

Hairpins
Thick paper or cardboard
P.V.A. glue
Silver or gold spray paint
Newspaper
Ribbon, about 20 cm in length

1. (Adult) cut two circles of paper about 3cm in diameter. Put glue in centre of circle and place about eight hairpins onto glue, leaving rounded ends touching in centre.

2. Glue ribbon to other paper circle. When glue and hairpins are almost set, place other circle of paper on top of pins, ribbon side down. Press firmly. Allow to dry.

3. (Adult) spread newspaper in well-ventilated area. Lay ornament on newspaper and spray with gold or silver paint. Allow to dry. Tie to Christmas tree.
For variation, paint hairpins with glue and roll them in glitter. Make other decorative shapes.

Note: Children under 4 may need help to arrange hairpins.

POLYSTYRENE TRAYS

Cut trays into Christmas shapes. They can be painted with thick powder paint to which dishwashing liquid is added. If the paint will not adhere to part of the tray, add more dishwashing liquid. Tissue paper may be stuck to the shapes with liquid starch. Trim when dry. If the tissue paper comes loose when it is dry, add a drop of P.V.A. glue.

POLYSTYRENE BALLS

Cover balls with foil and paint with thick paint mixed with dishwashing liquid or cover them with tissue paper applied with liquid starch. Set the balls on narrow necked bottles while decorating or allowing them to dry to prevent them rolling around.

Alternatively, decorate them by covering with P.V.A. glue (clear craft glue and spray enamel paint dissolves the balls) and rolling in glitter. Small cutout shapes of Christmas fabrics may be applied with P.V.A. glue. Sequins and small beads may be added to ball by putting them onto a pin with a large head and sticking it into the ball. Give them a finished look by wrapping a ribbon around in one direction, fastening it with a pin, wrapping it around in the other direction and pinning it. For hanging, pin a loop of ribbon on top or use a pipe cleaner. Make a small hole first with a toothpick and insert pipe cleaner.

'STAINED GLASS' SHAPES

Apply tissue scraps to waxed paper with liquid starch. Allow to dry. Cut Christmas shapes out of waxed paper, punch a hole in the top of shape and hang in front of a light on the tree.

CHRISTMAS CARDS

Old Christmas cards make delightful tree decorations and are easy to do. Simply cut out designs and figures from your favourite old cards, punch a hole through top of cutout, thread a colourful ribbon through hole and tie it onto tree.

SNOW FLAKES

YOU WILL NEED:

Colourful squares of thin paper (any size)
Scissors

1. Fold square in half then fold in half again. Two sides of the square will have only folds, no raw edges; fold these two sides together to make a triangle.

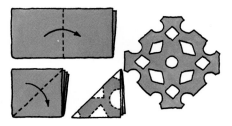

2. Around outside edges of shape, cut small V shapes, half circles or any designs so that there is a hole left where the shape is cut and the edges are no longer straight. Unfold paper for snowflake.

Older children can fold the squares into eighths or sixteenths to make a more intricate snowflake. Younger children may need help with cutting folded paper.

PRETZEL ORNAMENTS

YOU WILL NEED:

Pretzels
P.V.A. glue
Red and green crinkly gift wrapping ribbon or double-sided satin ribbon
Aluminium foil, about 15cm x 20cm piece

1. Place foil on table. Arrange pretzels into a design on the foil so that each pretzel touches another in at least two places.

2. Place one large drop of glue at each point where pretzels touch. When joined, add drop more glue.

3. Make sure all pretzels are touching in the glued areas. Leave on foil. Allow to dry overnight.

4. Remove ornament carefully from foil. Weave ribbon through holes. Handle the pretzel gently.

PAPER STARS

YOU WILL NEED:

Colourful squares of thin paper, about 20cm x 20cm
Scissors

1. Fold square in half diagonally to make a triangle. Mark centre point along fold (point A). Keeping first fold, fold twice more to make a triangle each time.

2. Fold top of triangle (point B) down as shown in illustration, taking care to line up folded edges evenly along bottom.

3. Cut away shaded area. Open paper out for an eight point star. Cut a jagged line or cut curves for flower shapes.

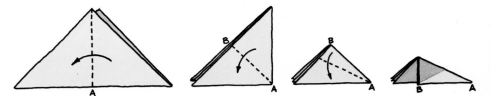

Candle centrepieces

YOU WILL NEED:

Uncooked salt play dough
(recipe, page 64)
Aluminium foil
Gum nuts, seed pods with
longish stems, small pine
cones, greenery sprigs
Red candles
Christmas ribbon
Silver or gold spray paint
Glitter
Bobby pins
Clear gloss enamel

1. Play dough will form the foundation for the centrepiece. Put play dough on piece of foil around a fat red candle or, for variation, keep play dough in a wreath shape and stick thinner red candles into it.

2. Push gum nuts and other items firmly into dough.

Be really original and spray cicada shells silver or gold!

3. If centrepiece is not to be painted, add ribbons tied in bows by sticking a bobby pin through back of bow and pushing the pin ends into the dough.

4. (Adult) if centrepiece is to be painted, remove candles. In a well-ventilated area, spray gold or silver paint onto centrepiece. Glitter may then be sprinkled on. (Adult) spray glitter with clear gloss enamel to keep it in place.

5. If desired, fold foil under dough after it is firm. Move centrepiece by placing a small plate next to it and pulling foil and centrepiece onto the plate gently.

'Stained glass' window

YOU WILL NEED:
Lightweight black paper
Same size sheets waxed paper,
tracing paper or any
transparent paper
Liquid starch in bowls
Paintbrushes
P.V.A. glue
Cellophane or tissue paper
torn into small pieces,
about 3cm to 8cm

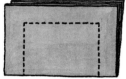

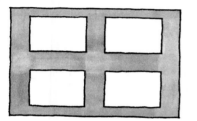

1. (Adult) fold heavy paper into eighths. On a side that has only folds (no raw edges), cut out a square as illustrated. When unfolded this is the window frame. The frames need not be square shapes. Snowflakes (page 121) would be very attractive.

2. Place waxed paper or tracing paper onto table. If it curls, tape corners to table. If using tissue paper, apply a little liquid starch to waxed paper and place tissue paper on it. If using cellophane, put glue around edges and place it on waxed paper. Liquid starch will make cellophane buckle.

3. Glue the frame onto the waxed paper or tracing paper. Hang on the window for the sun to shine through. Heavy white paper should replace the transparent paper if the picture is not to hang on a window.

Nature wreath

YOU WILL NEED:
2 sheets heavy cardboard
P.V.A. glue
Pine cones, gum nuts, seed pods, dried leaves
Christmas ribbon
Pencil
Large plate and smaller plate
Scissors

1. Make a wreath by tracing around a large plate on both cardboard sheets. Place a smaller plate in centre of drawn circle and trace around it on both sheets.

2. (Adult) cut out both pieces and glue them together for additional strength. For hanging, punch a small hole with scissors about one centimetre in from outside edge of cardboard circle.

3. With hole at top, glue pine cones, gum nuts, seed pods and other objects onto cardboard. Use glue generously.

4. (Adult) tie ribbon into bows, child can then glue them to wreath. Allow wreath to dry overnight. For a glossy effect, (adult) paint with clear gloss enamel.

Index

Musical instruments pages 103-105.

The majority of photographs in this book were taken by Jean Paul Ferrero/Auscape in Canberra and ACP photographer Andre Martin. Their photographs are supplemented by ACP staff members Russell Brooks, Ashley Mackevicius, Kevin Brown and Stuart Spence.

ACKNOWLEDGEMENTS
Our thanks to the children and staff at Duffy Preschool and Duffy Primary School, A.C.T. who made most of the art and craft projects in this book; to the children and staff at Birchgrove Community Preschool, Sydney, who made the koala piñata (page 101) and weaving project (page 37). Sykes Indoor Plant Services, Wahroonga, N.S.W. provided the Christmas tree; Bloomey's, Sydney, supplied some nature articles. Recipes were tested by Michelle Gorry of The Australian Women's Weekly Test Kitchen. Lettering by Brooke Stanford.